# Life Under
# a Leaky Roof

# Life
# Under
# a Leaky
# Roof

*Reflections on home, tools,*

*and life outside the big city*

## David Owen

**LF** LEBHAR-FRIEDMAN BOOKS
NEW YORK • CHICAGO • LOS ANGELES • LONDON • PARIS • TOKYO

LEBHAR-FRIEDMAN BOOKS
A company of Lebhar-Friedman, Inc.
425 Park Avenue, New York, New York 10022
*Visit our Web site at lfbooks.com*

Most of the stories in this collection were originally published, in different form, in *Home*. Others were published, in different form, in *The Atlantic Monthly, The New Republic, The New York Times Magazine,* and *Sports Illustrated*.

Library of Congress Cataloging-in-Publication data is available.
ISBN 0-86730-799-4

BOOK DESIGN AND COMPOSITION BY KEVIN HANEK
SET IN FF SCALA

Manufactured in the United States of America on acid-free paper

*For my mother*

# Contents

## AUTUMN

## WINTER

# Introduction

Aᴘ FRIEND RECENTLY MOVED FROM the West Coast to the East Coast. The change could not have been more extreme: from teeming city to tranquil suburb, from bungalow to mansion, from palm trees to ice dams, from old neighbors to new strangers. Despite the obvious changes, though, my friend himself felt oddly untransformed. His life had been turned upside down; why did everything feel the same?

"Oh, yeah," he realized. "*I'm* still here."

Our dwellings do change us, but the process takes time, and it's reciprocal: our houses remodel us as we remodel them. Home improvement is a kind of self-invention, and through it our walls, floors, and furniture become projections of our lives. Then we move on and others move in, and the process begins again.

The process for my wife and me began in 1985. I was walking down Park Avenue in New York City, where we had lived for eight years, when I ran into the father of a friend. He happened to mention that my friend and his wife had just bought a house in the country. My wife and I had always felt competitive with this couple, so news of their big purchase hit us hard. We had been meaning to move out of our cramped apartment and away from New York for some time, but we had never gotten around to it. Now we realized that we had to act.

A few days later, I rented a car, drove to a small Connecticut town where I had never set foot (but where my wife's stepgrandmother, coincidentally, had attended boarding school between 1919 and 1921), and called on a real estate agent whose name I had been given by a friend of a friend. The agent took me to look at a house. "I think it's too small," I said. The agent took me to look at another house. "I think it's big enough," I said. It had been built around 1790 and been added onto since, and like most old houses in New England it was painted white and had black shutters. During a period coinciding almost exactly with the history of the United States, it had served as a house, a social club, a prep-school dormitory, and a house again. In 1969 it had been cut in two, lifted from its foundation, and moved, on the back of a big truck, to its present site. The interior walls were covered with ugly wallpaper. The paint on the clapboards was peeling, the roof was leaking, and the garage was falling down. A dangerous-looking exterior staircase led from the back door to a third-floor apartment, which at that moment was occupied by a second-grade teacher and her husband. A long clothesline, sagging with the underwear of strangers, stretched between the back porch and a distant white pine.

I walked around the yard for a few minutes, looking at the house from various angles. I added up the rooms on my fingers. Then I said to the real estate agent, "I think I'd like to buy it." Her jaw dropped. She said, "Don't you think your wife ought to see it first?" I said, "Oh, I'm sure she'll like it." We went back to her office, where I signed a binder, and then she took me out to lunch.

That evening, I had trouble describing the house to my wife. (Our daughter was ten months old, and we had decided to spare her a long day in the car.) A few weeks later, we all drove up to take a look, but I couldn't find the house. In fact, I couldn't find the town. When I did find the house, my wife hated it. Because she hated it, I began to hate it, too. Even so, after talking things over back in New York that night, we decided to go ahead and buy it, probably because we believed that abandoning a house it had taken me a single morning to discover would be more complicated and inconvenient than living for the rest of our lives in a place we didn't like.

As luck would have it, both the house and the town have turned out to be pretty much exactly right for us. In fact, I can't conceive of living anywhere else. Dumb luck? Yes, of course. But not as dumb as you may think. Here's why: If you don't know what you really need—as my wife and I most certainly did not in those days—then simply having more information won't help you make a good decision. If I had been on my toes, I might have probed the chestnut beams with an ice pick, asked about local schools, researched comparable real estate sales, taken a closer look at the roof, opened the garage door, and inquired into the ownership of the wooded expanse across the road. But taking those sensible steps would not have enhanced my ability to make a sound decision, because at that time I would have had no idea how to interpret what I learned. Possessing additional information would only have made my wife and me less likely to do a thing that, it turned out later, was probably the right thing for us to do.

My wife's and my experience can be distilled into a universal law: Ignorant people are more likely to be smart by accident than to be smart on purpose. So why not take a chance every once in a while?

When my wife, our daughter, and I finally moved in, our new house seemed big, dark, empty, and frightening; it was still the home of the previous owners, even though their cars and furniture were gone. But then we began to pull the place apart and put it back together—to turn their house into ours. We took down the clothesline. We turned the third-floor apartment into offices for ourselves. We began stripping wallpaper. Our plans changed as we went along, and the house itself helped to change them. I learned how to use a reciprocating saw. We made friends. Our daughter grew old enough for nursery school. We had a son. I coached a T-ball team. My wife taught Sunday school. The old man who owned the woods across the road died and bequeathed his property to the local land trust. Through a series of accidents too complex to untangle, we began to become the people we had vaguely imagined we might be when we rashly decided to abandon our old life in New York.

In 1985 I was a stranger in my house, my town, and even in my life. More than a dozen years and many buckets of joint compound later, my house, my town, and my life are mine. This book is not really a home-improvement guide, and not really a memoir. It's a collection of stories, grouped by season, about a house that shaped four lives, and vice versa.

# SPRING

# Rich Man, Poor Man

I LIVE BETTER THAN MOST KINGS. For example, I live far more comfortably than William I, who conquered England almost a millennium ago but, for all his wealth and power, had nothing remotely resembling a flush toilet. An army of ruthless Normans and the blessing of Pope Alexander II? Yes, he had those things. Paper towels and a riding lawn mower? No. Although William was stupefyingly rich by the standard of his time, he seems starkly impoverished by the standard of mine. No seedless grapes, no Home Box Office, no pressure-treated lumber. How did he get by?

History books are filled with the names of supposedly wealthy people who, upon closer inspection, turn out to have been practically destitute in comparison with me. Alexander the Great couldn't buy cat food in bulk at Pet Nosh—something I do a couple of times a year. Czar Nicholas II lacked a compound-miter saw. Entire nations trembled before these powerful men, who nonetheless had to muddle through their lives without the most mundane of modern amenities. Think of poor little John D. Rockefeller: All the oil in the world couldn't buy him a large-screen TV.

Given how much better off I am than so many famous dead people, you'd think that I'd be content—not to say smug—about my present circumstances. I have triple-track storm windows;

Croesus did not. My minivan has a little compartment for storing a pair of sunglasses; Andrew Mellon didn't have a minivan.

Perversely, these thoughts don't fill me with joy. The trouble is that I, like most people, measure my prosperity by comparing it with that of other living persons: various neighbors, former high school classmates, certain television personalities, and so on. The covetousness I feel when I look at my friend Howard's new kitchen is not mitigated by my knowledge that no French monarch ever had a Corian clean-up sink or a refrigerator with glass doors. My pulsating showerhead alone would have made me the envy of many emperors, but I feel shabby when I look at Howard's built-in recycling bins.

You would think that simply not having bubonic plague would be enough to put most of us in cheerful moods—but no, we want a hot tub, too. There is really no such thing as a rising or falling standard of living. As the centuries go by, people simply find different reasons to feel grumpy. Every improvement in one's situation is negated by an equal or greater improvement in someone else's.

The easiest path to happiness, I guess, would be time travel. If I took everything I own right now and moved it back a few decades, I would have it made. My income doesn't quite get the job done at the moment, but in the year I was born it would have made me stinking rich. Latex paint, a VCR, stain-resistant carpeting, my cordless screwdriver, four-wheel drive, air-conditioning, no-iron fabrics, a laser printer—these relatively ordinary household articles would have vaulted me to the pinnacle of prosperity a mere half-century ago. World leaders would have sought my advice. Small children would have followed me down the street, clamoring for dimes.

Another way to achieve happiness would be to take an objective look at the things one actually does own and realize that they are pretty nice, even by contemporary standards. Howard's dishwasher is quieter than mine, and it doesn't force him to scrub his dishes in the sink before putting them in—but any dishwasher at all is still a good deal. My house is much smaller than the houses of many investment bankers, but even so, it has a lot more rooms than my wife and I are able to keep clean.

Besides, to people looking back at our era from a century or two in the future, those bankers' fancy countertops and my own worn Formica will probably seem equally shabby. I can't quite keep up with my neighbor right now. But just wait.

# The Best Room
# in the House

BUYING OUR HOUSE USED UP more than all our money, so my wife and I had to renovate a little at a time. The snailish pace of our home-improvement campaign discouraged me at first. Gradually, though, I became convinced that our poverty was serendipitous and that all remodeling projects should be incremental.

People with lots of money sometimes transform a house from top to bottom before they've spent a night inside. A couple from out of town did that with a nice old house not far from ours. They loved everything about the place, apparently, except its interior and exterior. Their first decorating step was to hire a crew of demolition workers, who attacked the place as though they believed that pirates had hidden treasure there. They pulled up floors. They pulled down ceilings. They threw doors out of windows. For more than a month, Dumpsters the size of train cars filled the driveway.

Soon the house was an empty box, which the people from out of town proceeded to fill all at once. New floors were laid, new walls were built, new doors were hung. Furniture arrived in semitrailers. The new owners didn't move in until everything was exactly the way they thought they wanted it, down to the flowers in the vase on the marble counter in the powder room.

Even if I had the money, I wouldn't treat a house that way. A house needs to be tried on and worn for a while. You can't just barge in and tell it what's what. Besides, if you do all your renovating at once, what do you have to look forward to? The ideal way to transform a house is one room at a time. Coincidentally, that's what my wife and I have done with ours.

Renovating incrementally has several advantages. One is that it is seemingly inexpensive. Instead of spending a million dollars all at once, the way those people from out of town did, you dribble away your bank's money a thousand bucks at a time. Writing lots of relatively small checks makes you feel wealthier than writing one big check would. Similarly, the best way to pay for a car would be with twenty-dollar bills, so that the transaction would make a more lasting impression.

A second advantage to renovating piecemeal is that you get to spend more time hanging around with contractors. One of the most satisfying experiences in life is to watch other people work while you are not working but should be. People who renovate all at once don't get to watch very much, because they typically have to live somewhere else while the work is being done. They don't get to look over the shoulders of their plumbers, or hold cables for their electricians, or play with their carpenters' miter saws after their carpenters have gone home. They get no entertainment value for their remodeling dollar.

A third advantage is that you don't need as much furniture when you decorate little by little. At any rate, that has been the case at our house. When my wife and I tackle a new room— something we seem to do every eighteen months or so—we don't buy new stuff for it. We just bring in stuff from whatever room we tackled before. When we redid our daughter's bedroom a few years ago, we moved in a nice old desk from a sitting room that we had redone a year or two before that. The desk looked great in our daughter's bedroom. It had also looked great in the sitting room, but the sitting room was old news by that point. Then, a year or so later, we redid our own bedroom. Naturally, we moved the desk from our daughter's bedroom into ours, where it once again looked fresh and interesting. We think of our house the way a nautilus thinks of its shell: The only relevant compartment is the current one.

The fourth and biggest advantage of renovating little by little is that by doing so you gain the benefit of your home's accumulated wisdom. Our house certainly knew better than we did. It knew, for example, that the kitchen and adjoining playroom should remain connected only by a small, windowlike pass-through, rather than by a door. If we had had the money, we would have added the door to avoid the inconvenience of having to walk down the hall and around a corner just to separate two quarreling children. What we didn't realize, and the house did, is that inconvenience is a two-way street. Children who have to walk around a corner and down the hall to pull at a grown-up's legs and whine will often decide it's easier to settle their disputes themselves.

Our house was also right about another room, the bathroom on the second floor. That was the most depressing room in the house when we bought the place. For one thing, it was too big. It had been converted from an eighteen-by-eighteen-foot bedroom many years before, and two or three normal-sized bathrooms could easily have been carved from it. For another thing, it was ugly. The floor was covered with blue vinyl-sheet flooring in a pattern that resembled plastic stones embedded in glue. The woodwork had been painted baby blue, and the walls were covered with shiny orange-, pink-, gold-, blue-, and ivory-flowered wallpaper that had been hung upside down. (The blossoms of the enormous orange roses drooped toward the ceiling.) My wife and I agreed that the bathroom would be the first room to go.

As it turned out, we were wrong. In fact, that bathroom is now the only room in our house that still looks the way it did when we bought the place. It has survived because it has turned out to be just about exactly suited to the way we live.

We first began to realize we might have misjudged the bathroom when we noticed that our daughter—who was a little over a year old when we moved in—liked to play there. The floor on one side of the room is raised about four inches to accommodate the plumbing, and she loved to walk up and down the small step between the two levels. (Real steps frightened her, but this one she could take on the fly.) She also loved arranging toy animals on the fake stones in the flooring and squeezing herself under the bottom shelf in the bathroom closet.

When we saw that the bathroom was temporarily too useful to gut, we began to decorate. We had an old green couch that didn't go with any of our other furniture, so we moved it in, along with an old sewing-machine table, a rocking chair, a couple of bookcases, and a whatnot that had belonged to my grandmother. On the wall above the couch we hung a large picture of some sheep, and on another wall we hung a small picture of some other sheep. When my parents cleaned out their attic and found an old gilt-framed oil painting of a barefoot peasant girl walking through a mountain pass, they sent it to us and we hung it over the toilet. When our refrigerator died, I took off the doors and put it next to the sink. We began to store towels, toilet paper, and bath toys on the shelves, and books in what used to be the freezer.

On winter evenings in those first years, the bathroom was often the warmest room in the house. The windows would steam up, and our dachshund would lean into the blast of the heater and fall asleep standing up. My wife or I would bathe our daughter while the other read a magazine on the couch. If our daughter was cranky, we might stretch bathtime all the way from dinner to bedtime. Sometimes we took dessert up to the bathroom, or even dinner.

When our daughter got a little older, she would sit on the step next to the dog and pretend to read books while my wife and I folded laundry. When we had friends over for dinner, we sometimes served cocktails in the bathroom while she had her bath. That way, neither my wife nor I had to miss out on the party.

A few months after our son was born, I screwed a big hook into the ceiling and hung a Jolly Jumper from it. He would bounce up and down while I took my morning shower, and his sister would spread her dolls and coloring books on the couch. When our house was full of guests one weekend and I couldn't use my third-floor office, I set up my laptop computer on the sewing-machine table and spread my papers on the toilet. When I had a bad cold, I spent the night on the old green couch so that my coughing wouldn't disturb my wife.

Much has changed since then. The kids are now too old for bath toys or coloring books, and a weight-lifting machine has taken the place of the couch. But the floor is still blue, and the wallpaper is still upside down, and we still keep our towels in a refrigerator. We're going to remodel. Not this year, probably. But next year for sure. Or, at any rate, the year after that.

# House of Dreams

WHEN I WAS IN third or fourth grade, I had competing career aspirations. I wanted to be the owner/builder of a two-person submarine, and I wanted to be an architect. Because fate is arbitrary and cruel, I became neither. After four years of college, I ended up in an entry-level (and, as it turned out, exit-level) job as a checker of facts at a weekly magazine. If we still named people after their occupations, people with the surname Factchecker would be lowlier and more contemptible than people named Stablemucker.

The other member of my submarine-design team was my friend John Ruth. He and I spent many rainy afternoons dreaming of undersea exploration, drawing cutaway views of the vessel we intended to build, and arguing about details. How many spear guns would we need? Would we steer with a steering wheel, a joystick, or a doorknob? How closely would our sub resemble a shark? Did it really need a ballast tank (as John Ruth contended), or could we cause it to dive or rise simply by aiming it down or up (my idea)? I had a box in my room in which I kept possible submarine parts, among them a broken wristwatch and the black top hat of a plastic snowman which to me looked like a control knob. One summer John Ruth's parents sent him to a camp that offered scuba diving—a prerequisite for minisub-piloting, we both agreed—and I became almost frantically depressed, because I believed I could never catch up.

My desire to build a submarine turned out to be less enduring than my desire to design houses, an ambition that lasted until eighth grade. My local newspaper had a weekly feature about home design, and every story included a floor plan. I saved the floor plans in a folder for inspiration. I did my own designing on graph paper, which I bought at the dime store, and I spent a lot of time worrying about the difference in thickness between interior and exterior walls. I also worried about arithmetic, which my grandmother told me architects had to understand.

My designs had a number of characteristic features, including secret passageways, random-width doors and windows, turrets with bedrooms in them, and irregularly shaped closets (to use up leftover space). I also was a big believer in swimming pools that you could dive into from a second-story window. Most of the designs I saw in the newspaper seemed stuffy by comparison; why would anyone design a house without some kind of tunnel? (After seeing the movie *The Great Escape,* I asked my parents if I could chop a hole in the foundation of our house and dig a tunnel to the basement of the house across the street. I wanted to ride through the tunnel by pulling myself along while lying on my stomach on my skateboard, and I wanted to get rid of the excavated dirt the way they did in the movie, by letting it dribble down my pants legs while I walked around our neighborhood. My parents vetoed all my ideas.)

Eventually, I decided that I didn't want to be an architect after all—probably because of the math requirement. But I still figured that I would design a house for myself as soon as I became old enough to own one. That didn't happen either, and it's probably just as well. From what I've seen, designing your own house is as bad an idea as doing your own dental work. I know two architects who have done it, and their houses are both pretty odd, to say the least. In one of the houses, the kitchen and living room are on the second floor, the master bedroom and a lap pool are on the first, and there's a shower at the foot of the basement stairs. Curious, no? The other house has one room that can be reached only from the yard, and a living room with a hammock suspended twenty feet above the floor.

The problem in both cases, I think, is that the architects had no clients and therefore no one to argue with as they worked out their designs. There was no dialogue, so the bad ideas weren't filtered out. When you build a big thing, you need somebody looking over your shoulder who can tell you that you don't need a twenty-five-foot-high semiconical ceiling in your garage (a feature I once saw in another architect's house). You need someone who has a different way of looking at the world. You need someone like John Ruth.

# Apprenticed to Myself

MANY DO-IT-YOURSELF PROJECTS would be more enjoyable if you didn't have to do them yourself. My father and I made that discovery several years ago, when we decided to hang a new medicine cabinet in the bathroom on the second floor of my house. We had everything we needed for the job except an inkling of how to do it.

Our main problem was our inability to find wall studs from which to hang the cabinet. Tapping the wall above the sink revealed nothing except, apparently, the lonely vacuum of outer space. After several minutes of fruitless searching, we began to suffer auditory hallucinations. "That's it, right there," my father said. I drove an exploratory nail; the nail hit nothing. More tapping. "Oh, wait, it's over here," I said. Another nail. Again, nothing.

We began driving nails at random. A dozen nails, no stud. I took a finishing nail and used it to punch holes, sewing-machine style, at half-inch intervals. I drove close to a hundred holes but found no stud. "I don't think there *are* any studs," my father finally said, a great weariness in his voice.

As it turned out, he was almost right. In desperation, we used a keyhole saw to cut a foot-square hole above the sink. Shining a flashlight into the darkness, we discovered that the wallboard had been attached not to vertical studs but to horizontal strapping, which had been laid across the studs. We had driven all of our nails into the space between two pieces of strapping, and none of the nails had been long enough.

From that point onward, the project went fairly well. In fact, the strapping made an ideal backing for the medicine cabinet when we finally got around to hanging it, because it ran the width of the cabinet at pretty much the right height. (Other problems, too numerous to mention, delayed the installation; what we had thought would be a quick before-lunch bathroom enhancement ended up lasting until dinnertime.) But I feel embarrassed whenever I think about all those nail holes, and I feel doubly embarrassed when I think about that foot-square hole.

Do professional medicine-cabinet installers make Swiss cheese of the walls on which they do their installations? I doubt it. Will the future owners of this house laugh when they replace the cabinet and discover my perforations? I'm afraid they will.

We learn by doing, unfortunately. How much simpler life would be if we could learn by, say, drinking beer and watching football on TV. The problem that most do-it-yourselfers face is how to acquire home-improvement skills without ruining the home they are trying to improve. If one were young and living in the olden days, one could become an indentured servant of some kind. But one is just a regular late-twentieth-century guy with kids, a mortgage, and a job. What the heck is one supposed to do?

Well, I've thought about this a lot during the years since my father and I hung that medicine cabinet, and I have a few ideas. It is possible, I now believe, to acquire quite a few home-improvement skills by becoming, in effect, one's own apprentice.

My self-apprenticeship has taken many forms over the years. I learned about platform framing by building a tree house for my children. I learned how to measure and cut rafters by helping to build some playground equipment at my children's school. I practiced my roofing skills by building a house for my cat. I learned how to build a porch by rebuilding the steps in front of my house. I learned how to frame a partition by building stud walls in my basement. I learned how to lay tile by helping a friend tile his bathroom. I learned how to solder joints in copper pipe by trading an old wood-burning furnace I owned for plumbing lessons.

My education has taken longer than it would have if I had majored in home improvement in college. But I've had a good time learning the few skills I now possess, and I have a tree house, new front steps, and a dry cat to boot. There are still plenty of jobs that I don't feel qualified to tackle. But with a few more years of practice, I'll be ready to approach my wife with an idea I've been mulling over lately: dismantling our house down to the foundation and building a new one from scratch.

# Resale Values

THE EASIEST WAY TO INCREASE the value of your house by twenty-five thousand dollars is to add a fifty-thousand-dollar kitchen to it. Throw in a Jacuzzi, a personal sauna, an indoor lap pool, and a couple of bidets, and you might even come close to getting back what you paid for the place five years ago.

Sixty-two percent of all home-improvement projects are undertaken during the last six months before a house is sold. I just made up that statistic, but it sounds plausible. It is human nature not to think seriously about home improvement until it's time to move. When people fix up their houses, they tend to do so not to increase their own comfort but to impress potential buyers, whose standards, they figure, are higher.

Some friends of mine had all their floors refinished a few years ago. They did so not because they were tired of walking on crummy floors—they weren't—but because they were planning to move and their real estate agent had told them that shiny new floors would look a lot better to the total strangers who would soon be sizing up their house. My friends endured two weeks of dust, bad smells, and dislocated furniture—inconveniences that the real estate agent felt the new owners should be spared. All told, my friends got to enjoy their shiny new floors for about six months, or roughly five percent of the total time they owned their house.

Often, such desperate and expensive efforts to impress total strangers are fruitless. Some other people I know installed an expensive new kitchen in their house just before putting the place on the market. They figured that a house with a regular kitchen would be worth less than a house with polished-granite counters. The house sold a short time after the job was finished. One of the first acts of the new owners was to tear out the new kitchen and install a newer one. They even used the same contractor.

Moving is a tough way to get rich under any circumstances. (Just about the only way to do it is to sell a house in Pacific Palisades in order to buy one in Dubuque.) The transaction itself can burn up many years' worth of appreciation. There are fees for brokers, bankers, lawyers, inspectors, insurance companies, and, for all you can tell, the president of Mars. Forking over so much money in such a short period of time is both frightening and exhilarating. Until the moment we closed on our house, I hadn't realized that I was rich enough to write so many zeros on so many checks. Then, a moment later, I was back to being poor.

In the end, the houses that best retain their value are the ones that feel right to the people who live in them. What's the point of impressing potential buyers if you have to sacrifice your own comfort in order to do so? Besides, if the people who buy your house don't like your kitchen counters, they can always replace them—say, the week before they move out.

# My Decorators

A FRIEND ONCE ASKED MY WIFE AND ME if we had used a decorator when we fixed up our house. I said no, but I later realized I was wrong. We had a decorating team named Matz and Owen. They were my grandmothers.

My grandmothers never saw my house. But when they died, both well into their nineties, I inherited some of their furniture. Almost every room contains something that one or the other of them once owned. They helped to furnish my house, and as I walk through it I think of them.

My grandmother Owen was called Gaga. She was the first adult I was taller than. I used to love to spend the night at her house, because there was a huge pot in her kitchen cupboard in which she kept all the kinds of candy I liked best. I would sprawl on the big Oriental rug in her living room, eating Milky Ways and watching *The Jackie Gleason Show* on her color TV, which was the first color TV owned by anyone I knew. Today her living room rug is my living room rug. If I get down on my hands and knees, I can find particular worn spots that I used to notice as I worked my way through her collection of *National Geographics*. I can also find the parts of the pattern that I used as roadways and parking lots for my Matchbox cars.

As Gaga got older, her mind began to falter. One day my sister and I found that she had set five places at the table in her dining room. There were four places set in the usual way, and one right in the middle, where a centerpiece might go. "Who is that place for, Gaga?" my sister asked. Gaga looked puzzled, then laughed a little nervously and said, "Why, I don't know." Today that table is on my screened porch.

Gaga grew up on a farm in Indiana. Her parents called her Nellie, but she hated that name and changed it, when she was nine or ten years old, by crossing it out on her birth certificate and writing in "Mary Helen," the name she used from then on. She was a gardener and a Christian Scientist. When I broke my wrist in college, while dancing on a mantelpiece in a tuxedo, she visited a Christian Science practitioner, and the two of them focused healing thoughts on my fractured carpals. (When my cast came off, I told the doctor that my recently broken wrist wouldn't bend as far as the other one. The doctor pointed to the recently broken wrist and said, "This is normal. The other one bends too much.") Gaga also gave her practitioner credit for getting me into college in the first place, and for most of the other good fortune that my family enjoyed.

My grandmother Matz was called Grandmother. That name was contrived for her hastily one day when I referred to her as Mrs. Matz. I was two, and that was all I'd ever heard anyone call her. She was formal and somewhat frightening. My principal legacy from her is an old desk that belonged to my grandfather, who died before I was born. His portrait, which used to hang in her dining room, now hangs in mine. His desk supposedly has a secret compartment. As a boy, I spent many hours happily searching for it, tapping panels and measuring drawers, imagining the treasure it must contain. My own children search for that treasure now.

Toward the end of her life, Grandmother had a nurse who smoked cigarettes, and she would ask the nurse to come into her bedroom and blow smoke under the canopy of her bed. (My grandfather had been a smoker, and she missed the smell.) That bed, which had belonged originally to my great-grandmother, is now my daughter's. Grandmother herself toyed with smoking occasionally, in the same way teenagers do. I once opened a drawer in a side table in her living room and found an ashtray containing four cigarettes stubbed out after one or two puffs. That side table is now mine.

Grandmother grew up in Austin, Texas. She spent one summer at a camp in Maine but refused to swim in the cold water and so was rowed across the lake once a week for a hot bath at a nearby inn. Later she attended Miss Porter's School in Farmington, Connecticut—about an hour from where I live now—where the dour headmistress interrupted a Sunday-evening Scripture reading "so that the young lady from Texas may see her first snowfall." As a grown-up, she often drove back to Texas from Kansas City, where she had moved in 1921. During those trips, she invariably stopped to use the rest room at a particular Texaco station on the border between Kansas and Oklahoma. The owner of the station saw her so often he assumed she lived nearby. She told him she stopped at his gas station because he had the nicest ladies' room she had ever seen on a highway. On the basis of that, they exchanged Christmas cards for many years.

My grandmothers didn't always like each other; they were too different. Still, in some of my happiest memories they are together. I think especially of a cold Thanksgiving night when we were driving back from a big dinner at the country club. My father and mother were in the front seat. My sister and I were in the middle of the backseat, snuggled between our grandmothers. We could tell them apart in the dark by the texture of their fur coats. (Gaga's coat was soft, as she was. Grandmother's felt rougher.) My sister and I would bury our faces in their coats and try to guess when our car had turned onto our street, while my father tricked us by making unnecessary turns. I liked being surrounded by my grandmothers then, and I like being surrounded by them now.

# The Big Question

"CAN YOU HOLD THINGS when you're dead?"
"Daddy, is cheese vegetables, or what is it?"
"Why am I not a grown-up? I've been here for so many years."

These questions aren't the big question; they're just regular questions. You can answer them while parallel parking or while holding a crying baby in one arm and trying to use the cardboard tube from a roll of paper towels to scoop up ten pounds of spilled birdseed after tipping over the birdseed container while trying to move it someplace where it would be less likely to tip over. The exact wording of your answer makes no difference. Responding incorrectly will not condemn the four-year-old asker to decades of fruitless interrogation by psychotherapists.

Here's the big question: "How do babies get started?"

For various psychological reasons, most people feel uncomfortable describing sexual intercourse to young children. Given that fact, you'd think that grown-ups would have agreed long ago on a standard explanation that could be printed in several languages on small cards and, say, tucked into people's phone bills every month. When a child asked the big question, you could hunt up one of the cards in the pile of stuff on your desk and read the explanation in the same halting monotone that police officers use to inform suspected criminals of their rights. If a child felt cheated by this skimpy dodge, you could shrug and say, "Gee, this is the only card they gave us."

"Why don't you ask your mother someday when the two of you are standing in the checkout line at Stop & Shop?" is another possible response. (Or, "Hey, I was just about to ask you the same thing!") But evasion merely postpones the day of reckoning. The time always comes—as it did in our house a number of years ago—when the big question must be met directly.

"Well uh, a baby starts from a tiny, tiny egg, much smaller than the eggs in the refrigerator, uh, uh—honey?"

"Yes, well, uh, yeah, there's this special place inside the mom, and—gee, what say we go get some ice cream?"

All the experts say you don't need to give young children more information than they're really looking for. People who haven't graduated from nursery school don't want or need to know about the part played by popular music and aftershave lotion. Just give them the same sort of innocently inadequate answer you'd give if they asked how the TV works.

The trouble is that young children are too inquisitive and too observant to be satisfied for long with vague half-truths. They want hard facts. When my sister was dressing for a party once, her three-year-old son came into the room and demanded, "Turn around and let me see that no-penis." When my daughter was four, she asked me if her brother, who was one, had a tongue. I said that he did. She asked, "Did he have a tongue when he was born?" I said yes. She asked, "Did he have a tongue when the egg and the seed came together?" I said, "No, not yet." You can't buy off people like that with stories about the stork.

For various psychological reasons, I feel uncomfortable recounting exactly what my wife and I told our children. I will say only that we gave them a heck of a lot more information than my parents gave me, and that they took it right in stride and went on with their lives. My son, at the age of three or so, quietly considered what I had told him, and then asked, "Was it gwoss?"

One thing I realized while wrestling with the big question is how essentially unbelievable the big answer is. The way plants get started is fairly plausible; the way people get started is not. It sounds like science fiction. And the most remarkable thing about it is that you scarcely have a chance to catch your breath before the result of it is cornering you in the kitchen and asking you to explain the trick.

# Working at Home

ONE OF THE GREAT ADVANTAGES of working at home is that your time is your own. One of the great disadvantages is that you have to devote quite a bit of that time to making the other members of your family think you are working when in fact you are just balancing a pencil between your lip and the base of your nose, studying the miniature newsletter that came with the electric bill, or practicing your golf swing.

When my friend Jim graduated from college, he briefly worked for his father, who made his living buying and selling stocks. Jim's father worked out of the family's dining room, which was so cluttered with papers that there was no room in it for anyone but him, and certainly no room for dining. As a result, Jim had to work in his own bedroom. That was fine with Jim, because Jim had no great interest in working to begin with. He had taken the job with his father only because his father had insisted that he not just sit around for the rest of his life, even though that had pretty much been his major in college. Every morning, Jim would close the door of his bedroom, open the top drawer of his dresser, stretch out on his bed with that day's *Wall Street Journal* spread across his lap, and go to sleep. If his father came to his room to ask him something, the opening door would strike the dresser drawer, making a loud sound that would startle Jim, who would open his eyes and pretend to be trying to understand what debentures are. That went on for about a week. Then Jim's father got wise and sent him to business school.

Making my children think I am working is easy; for all they know, leaning way back in a chair and changing channels with a remote control really is a kind of job. Fooling my wife is harder, because she also works at home, and her office is next to mine. When the typing in my office stops, she knows that I have subtly shifted the responsibility for paying our mortgage over to her; when I hear her chair gently creaking in a particular way, I know that she has fallen asleep.

My wife's and my offices are on the third floor of our house. That means that going down to the kitchen to make a cup of coffee or eat a few of the children's Fruit Roll Ups can be quite a time-consuming process. Typically, I like to work for a good quarter-hour before I even begin to think of going down to the kitchen. And as long as I am downstairs, I might as well start a load of laundry. And as long as I am doing that, I might as well let the dog out. And as long as I am doing that, I might as well go for a walk.

# On the Level

L IKE MANY MEN, I take frequent breaks during the day in order to putt golf balls on the carpeted floor of my office. Unlike most men, I have an office that is ideally suited to golf. The floor runs steeply downhill from the southern wall—the drop is three inches—then rises gently toward the northern wall. The floor also sags along the line running from the southeast corner to the northwest corner. As a result, I am able to practice not only uphill and downhill putts, but also putts that break to the right and left. My putting, not surprisingly, has become pretty good. Indeed, there are those who say it is the bedrock of my game.

Building an indoor putting facility as fancy as mine would cost a lot of money if you had to do it from scratch. But I didn't have to pay anything for mine: it was already here when we moved in. In fact, my wife and I (like many old-house owners) have something of an embarrassment of riches as far as interior topography is concerned. The floor in our bedroom, for example, is so steeply tilted that unattended shoes sometimes slide under the bed—in effect, putting themselves away. My children are quick and agile because when they were little they had to learn to keep their balance while running in stockinged feet down the steeply pitched hallway that leads to their playroom. Best of all, we never have to remember to close the door of our refrigerator, because the kitchen floor slopes toward the wall behind it, permitting gravity to take over when we release the handle.

Corners that aren't square and walls that aren't plumb are another attractive feature of our house. The lopsidedness of every visible surface provides a comfortable margin of error for my adventures in carpentry and cabinetmaking. When I build a bookcase, I don't have to worry that the right side is a little bit taller than the left side, or that I could squeeze not only a razor blade but most of my razor into the gaps between the trim pieces. My sloppy, ill-conceived home-improvement projects would look terrible in a brand-new house, where every line would be parallel or perpendicular to every other, but they look fine in mine. A perfectly level surface in my house would disorient a sensitive visitor, and might even be dangerous for someone with an inner-ear disorder.

Admittedly, living in an old house poses difficulties as well. Every day, it seems, there are new decisions to be made. When I hang a picture, should I line it up with the ceiling or the floor? Should I prop up the legs on the downhill side of our bed, or saw off the legs on the uphill side? When I remodel our kitchen, should I align the new counter with true level (in which case it will appear to be slanted) or with apparent level (in which case water from the drainboard will run onto the floor)? Is it absolutely necessary for a door to close (or, depending on the season, to open)?

On the whole, I guess, the advantages of old-house living outweigh the disadvantages. Explaining continental drift to my children was a snap (the mattresses on their beds are continually, imperceptibly sliding toward their bedroom doors). Grapes that fall from our kitchen table inevitably roll to a single, convenient collection point near the radiator under the microwave. (The tendency of spilled food to end up in one spot also makes life easier for our dog.) If I ever have to spend the night on a ledge on the face of a mountain, I won't worry, because I've become good at gripping my bedding with my toes while I sleep. And, best of all, my golf handicap is lower than it's ever been. Who cares if those hills visible in the distance through our living room windows appear to be listing slightly to the right?

# Where the Sun
# Never Shines

**M**Y GARAGE MAKES ME UNEASY. In theory, it is a three-car garage; in practice, it can hold about a car and a half. The rest of the space is taken up by various items, some of them quite large. Recently, I explored the garage with a flashlight—there are lights on the outside but none on the inside—and found the following:

- Approximately two cubic yards of broken bricks. When we moved into our house, there was a big brick barbecue in the backyard. It looked like a sacrificial altar, or a brick telephone booth lying on its side. Reducing it to a pile of rubble took me two full days with a sledgehammer. Because I couldn't think of anything to do with the rubble, I hauled it into the garage and dumped it against the rear wall, which for a number of years had been bowing inward under the weight of the big, wet hill behind it. Later, I threw an old toilet onto the pile, too.

- All our bicycles, all our rakes and shovels, two of my six golf bags, and twelve fifty-five-gallon garbage cans. We have more garbage cans than anyone I know, perhaps because my wife and I both work at home in addition to living here and so produce more trash. We sometimes have to tape money to one of the barrels so that the garbage man will empty them all.

- A community of squirrels and *their* refuse (mostly chewed-up pinecones).

- A washer and drier. These were part of the house when we bought it, but they stopped working almost immediately, so I put them in the garage and began piling junk on them. The junk now includes flowerpots, hedge clippers, a broken sled, a can of thawing lubricant, some firewood that someone gave me, and one end of a big aluminum rake, which I use to scrape snow off my roof.

- A house for our cats. I am allergic, so our cats can't live indoors. I built a house for them and put it by our back door, but one winter my wife began to worry that the cats didn't recognize it as a shelter, so she bought them another house and put it in the garage. The new house replaced an improvised winter refuge, which I had pieced together from old foam couch cushions, a big cardboard box, and a small, colorful tent my children used to play in. The cats never used my improvised shelter, and they don't use the new house, either, but we still keep both structures in the garage.

- A big broken plastic swimming pool filled with small broken plastic things. The swimming pool bridges the gap between the pile of broken bricks and the last of a cord of firewood that I bought in 1986 from a guy who said he would stack it neatly in the garage but dumped it in the driveway and drove off as soon as I had paid him. If you don't hear the side of the swimming pool crumple slightly as you park the minivan, then you haven't pulled the minivan far enough into the garage to close the door behind it.

Cleaning up all these things would be impossible. The only container big enough to hold them would be another garage, and we don't have two. I'll tell you one thing, though. I've stopped making fun of people who have old cars in their front yards.

# True Comfort

**M**Y FATHER OWNED A SUCCESSION of large recreational vehicles during the years when I was growing up. Each was bigger and more luxurious than its predecessor, and each was referred to by our family as the Bus. Occasionally, I was allowed to drive the Bus. A few times I borrowed it for a date. The look on the face of a mother whose daughter is being swept off to a drive-in movie by a high school junior driving a Greyhound-sized motor home is beyond the power of language to describe.

The feature of the Bus that I liked best was its potent ambiance of cozy self-containment. If the living rooms in people's houses measured just seven feet by ten feet, as did the sitting area in the Bus, then modern life would not be the icy wasteland of misapprehended silences that in the opinion of some people it is.

If I were interested only in my own comfort, and not in what other people think of me, the living room in my house might look pretty much exactly like the sitting area in the Bus. In other words, it would not look like some unexplored tributary of Carlsbad Caverns. (I have caught bats in my living room. But that's another story.) The sitting area of the Bus, which was furnished only with a built-in couch and several built-in swivel chairs, was just big enough to accommodate six or eight slightly inebriated adults and their drinks. That, it seems to me, is also the ideal size for a living room. It precludes the possibility of big, noisy parties.

Another comfortable feature of the Bus: it had wall-to-wall carpeting. My house doesn't. Instead, it has beautiful eighteenth-century pine and chestnut floors. The floors are the kind that old-house lovers remorselessly kill for, but they are not, to be perfectly honest, comfortable. They are bumpy and uneven, and in the winter they are cold. When my children were little, they would sometimes catch their toes in the gaps between the boards. (Before we finally carpeted our stairs, my daughter, who was two, asked, "Why don't we have soft stairs, like Grammie and Pa?")

The floors in my house are considerably less comfortable than, for example, the floors in a crummy motel room. Once, I stayed in a crummy motel room where the wall-to-wall carpeting ran all the way up one of the walls. It was darned comfortable. The ideal bedroom, I think, would be a lot like that. It would have an extra bed that you could throw your stuff on. It would have a big mirror positioned so that you could watch yourself watching the big TV. And it would have wall-to-wall carpeting on the walls.

The most comfortable room I've ever been in was a college-library reading room that had big, deep, down-filled, leather-upholstered armchairs. You were supposed to place a plank across the arms of your chair and spread your books on that. No one ever did much work in those chairs, however, because the cushions were so soft that by the time you stopped sinking into them your books were on a level with your chin. Like most people, I did my studying in my dorm room and went to the library only to sleep. As I dozed off, I had a dim awareness of a slowly turning fan up on the ceiling, and of the hum of quiet voices near me, and of the soft, well-padded carpet under my feet.

# The Living Room Problem

HE ROOM THAT PEOPLE NOWADAYS call the living room has always been a problem. In the nineteenth century, when it was known as the parlor, it was often associated less with living than with dying, since it was the room where departed family members were laid out. The name "living room" was coined at the turn of the century by *Ladies' Home Journal,* whose editors felt that a change in labeling might dispel some of the Victorian gloom with which the parlor had become shrouded.

My wife and I never held a funeral in our living room, but during the first ten years we owned our house, a coffin would have been in keeping with the decor. Like most people, we set foot in our living room in those days only to open Christmas presents and vacuum. There was something about the place that defied occupancy. For one thing, it was too big. It had been created in the early part of the twentieth century when some earlier owner had merged the front and rear parlors by removing two massive fireplaces, which had separated the two rooms for the previous hundred and twenty years. The resulting space was about thirty feet by fifteen feet—smaller than Grand Central Station but nearly as large as the apartment where my wife and I began our married life. It would have been a good place to hold a dancing school—as someone did during the twenties and thirties—but it was a forbidding place to read a magazine.

During the first year we lived in our house, we used the living room mainly to store boxes, which we had been too lazy to unpack after moving in. In weak moments, we half considered leaving the boxes there permanently. After all, the living room was more accessible than either the attic or the basement, and it was nice and dry. We could have added some sturdy metal shelving from Sears and had a good place to keep beach toys during the winter. But we kept being brought up short by the same chilling question: What would our mothers say?

Modern Americans tend to do most of their "living" either in the kitchen or in an adjoining family room or great room. In newer houses, the family room is typically the size and shape of a church, and it is usually dominated by an enormous TV. (In some new houses, you get the feeling that the TV was bought first, and the house designed around it.) The living room, if there is one, tends to be vestigial.

My house doesn't have a family room, although it does have both a playroom and a book-and-TV-filled den, which we call the library. The library opens off one end of the living room, and it is everything that the living room originally was not: cozy, inviting, used. My wife and I used to spend so much time in the library and so little time in the living room that I began to think of the living room less as an actual room than as a tasteful painting that hung on one wall of the library: still life with white couch and fireplace tools.

After a decade of brooding, though, my wife and I decided that the time had come to try to turn the living room into a place where someone other than our house cleaner might occasionally be tempted to set foot. Our first move was to buy some more comfortable furniture. The key piece was a new couch, and it made a big difference. The new couch is long enough to take a nap on, and, unlike the old couch, it's soft enough to sit on without making you think you're doing something good for your posture. A few days after it was delivered, I spotted our dog curled up on it—the definitive endorsement. We also bought some comfortable chairs, replaced the coffee table with a big ottoman, moved the piano to a better place, and bought some better lamps.

The most important and expensive element in our improvement scheme was the addition of built-in bookcases. The cabinetry was designed by one neighbor and constructed by another, and it performed the seemingly miraculous trick of humanizing the scale of the room. We now spend so much time in there that I occasionally worry we are neglecting the library.

Some people were surprised that we added bookcases, because they figured we already had more than enough places to store books. There are built-in bookcases in the library, the kitchen, the playroom, my office, and the basement, and there are freestanding bookcases in all the bedrooms, the porch, the bathroom, and just about everywhere else. But all those shelves had been overflowing for some time. After your book collection crosses a certain threshold, it begins to reproduce by itself. Detective novels, golf-instruction books, and the *Baby-Sitters Club* seem to be especially fertile.

A more practical approach might have been to do some serious weeding. Do I really need three copies of a novel I hated in high school and haven't looked at since? Wouldn't the local library be a more logical home for picture books that our kids have outgrown? Will I ever take another run at my twelve-volume unabridged edition of the diary of Samuel Pepys? The likely answers are no, yes, and no. But I don't think I could ever make myself get rid of books—at least not hardcovers. Even when I'm not reading them, I like to know they're there, emitting knowledge molecules into the air. I also like to see them. A wall covered with books has the same enticingly intricate visual impact as a floor covered with an Oriental rug. It's like a huge, complicated flower arrangement that you don't have to water.

Eventually, of course, the new bookcases will overflow as well. But there is a little more empty wall space in the living room, not to mention all that empty space in the middle of the floor. And if our book collection grows to the point where even the living room begins to seem too small, we can always knock out a wall and add on.

# Front and Back

WHEN MY CHILDREN WERE LITTLE, I worried that they might be directionally challenged. One day, I asked them to open the front door so that I could carry some lumber straight up the stairs to the second floor. The door was locked when I got there, a stack of two-by-fours teetering on my shoulder. I looked through the window: no kids. I put down my load and found my kids on the other side of the house, waiting for me next to the washing machine.

Then it came to me: the laundry-room door was the one we always used, and it was the door that was closest to the driveway. How could that door not be the front?

Confusion about front and back is not unique to my family. Many American houses have front doors that, like neckties and belly buttons, serve no obvious purpose. I even know a guy whose front door has wallboard on the other side: the previous owners sealed it up in order to make more space for their living room couch. I asked him what he does when people come to the phony door and knock. "In fifteen years," he said, "it's happened twice." Both times, he added, the person who knocked was wearing a dark suit and a skinny tie and was carrying an armful of religious pamphlets.

Just about the only people who ever knock on my front door are dinner guests. A dinner party is a special occasion—and, at our house, an increasingly rare one—and some people feel that special occasions call for special doors. Wading through the herd of sneakers and roller skates on the floor of the laundry room wouldn't seem festive, these people decide. So they hike halfway around the house and knock on a door I never think to answer. The dog hears the knocking and begins to bark—but at the other door.

My door problem is compounded by the fact that the front of my house seems to most people to be around back. When the previous owner had the house moved here from up near the village green, he oriented it so that the front door faced the nearest principal road. A good idea—except that the nearest principal road is way down at the bottom of the hill, past some trees and on the other side of a creek, and you can't see it in the summer, and our driveway connects not to it but to a little dirt road that runs parallel to the side of the house. From the driveway, the door you see is the one the dog thinks is the only one worth worrying about.

In new construction, architects sometimes throw up their hands and put all the doors on the same side of the house. We have a neighbor whose house, at first glance, seems to have two front doors, roughly twenty feet apart. But you can easily tell which one you are supposed to use. The door on the left leads into the kitchen and is for friends; the door on the right leads into the front hall and is for party guests and itinerant evangelists. I use the door on the left if I'm just dropping by and the door on the right if I was invited by mail.

Still other people deal with the door problem by ignoring front and back and using the big door only. That is, they come and go through their garage. My sister has a house like that. Her two-car garage is really her foyer, and her automatic opener is her key. She has perfectly nice front and back doors, too, of course. But the entrance that gets the most use is the one with oil stains on the floor.

# Tub People

I TURNED ONE OF THE FULL BATHS in my house into a half-bath. I did it by moving my children's red-eared turtle into the tub, which then became useless for any other purpose. The turtle had previously lived in a ten-gallon tank in the middle of our kitchen table, where it had been responsible for a bad smell. Eventually, we realized that the bad smell would not go away unless we cleaned the turtle's tank daily—obviously an impossibility in a household where toys are not put away but rather piled like hay in the corners of various rooms. In the tub, the turtle can be hosed down hourly, if needed. All you have to do is turn on the water and pull the plug.

The bathroom that the turtle now occupies is on the ground floor of my house, roughly equidistant between the laundry room and the kitchen, many miles from the nearest bedroom. There is no reason for a bathroom in such a location to have a bathtub in it, unless the bathroom was once a bathroom in a dormitory for a boys' boarding school, as this one was. (My house was a dorm during the forties, fifties, and sixties. The bathroom on the second floor once had five urinals and a walk-in shower.) That ground-floor bathtub had always seemed like a silly waste of space to me. Because it takes up so much room, the sink and the toilet are crammed together. In fact, you have to turn kind of sideways to get past the sink to the toilet. But as soon as the turtle moved in, I began to miss the tub.

I didn't miss it because I missed taking baths in it. The only member of our family who has ever bathed in that tub is the dog. But I miss bathing the dog. A bathtub near the back door is a handy amenity if your dog is low to the ground and, therefore, close to the mud. I used to be able to grab the dog on the back step, take three or four big strides, and drop it into the tub almost before it knew I had it. Now I have to lug it upstairs to a tub that people use, and long before I get there the dog has figured out what's going on. Our dog is small, but it can develop a lot of torque. The whole process was easier in the days before we had a pet that requires, in effect, around-the-clock bathing.

Another thing I miss is the ability to chill down several cases of beer, a suckling pig, a box of lobsters, or anything else too big to fit into the refrigerator. (Almost anything is too big to fit into our refrigerator. We put away food the way the Japanese load subway trains.) I used to be able to throw big stuff into the tub and cover it with ice. During parties, that bathroom became a sort of centralized beer-processing station: you could pick up a new beer at the same time you were dropping off the old one.

Our old turtle-free bathtub was so handy that I almost think everyone should have a tub near the kitchen—maybe even in the kitchen. That would make it easier to thaw turkeys and to clean up children after meals. In fact, you could eliminate all the intermediate steps and feed the kids right in the tub.

The turtle, during meals, could live in the sink.

# Handyman Special

**M**Y FRIENDS JIM AND JANE bought a ninety-year-old farmhouse that had been on the market for several years. They now face a daunting home-improvement campaign that will probably last for decades and may cost them their marriage, but I think they made the right decision. The house is in rough shape—leaky roof, exhausted paint, nasty bathrooms, plywood floor in the kitchen—but it sits on a nice piece of property in an area where houses in good condition sell for two or three times what Jim and Jane paid for theirs. With just a couple of weeks of furious activity and a dozen or so trips to the dump, they have already succeeded in making the place look much worse—the crucial first step in any successful renovation. Best of all, Jim and Jane's purchase has turned out to be a good deal for my friend Bill and me.

Bill is a lawyer who worked his way through law school as a carpenter. Like me, he has just about finished fixing up his own old house. Our walls are patched, our floors are finished, and our roofs no longer leak. Helping out at Jim and Jane's place has let us both get our hands dirty again, but without getting our rugs dirty as well.

Our main task recently has been undoing damage done by the previous owners. Their most conspicuous addition was a large, featureless deck just outside the living room. The deck was your standard handyman special: a small forest's worth of greenish, poison-impregnated lumber hovering a couple of feet above the ground. It had no railing and no steps down to the yard. Jim and Jane hated it on sight—then noticed that the underside looked odd. Jim poked around with a flashlight and discovered that the deck had been built directly on top of a nice old stone patio surrounded by a low stone wall. Bill and I helped Jim tear out the deck, liberating the patio.

Poor remodeling decisions are not a modern invention. The second floor of Jim and Jane's house was blighted by dreary plywood paneling, which had been added in the late forties or early fifties—the golden age of cross-laminated wood veneer. The plywood covered every surface, including the ceilings. Late one afternoon, Bill and I pried off a small section over a doorway and showed Jim and Jane what was hiding underneath: reasonably sound plaster walls and nice nineteenth-century beaded door and window casings. In a couple of hours we had pulled down all the plywood and tossed it out a window into the back of Jim's pickup truck. The newly exposed plaster needed patching, and the trim needed paint, but the house immediately looked bigger, brighter, and more inviting. Next job on the list: pulling up the fifties-era linoleum tiles, which conceal a nice old pine floor in the hall.

Jim and Jane alternate between feeling exhilarated by the idea that they got a bargain and depressed by the realization that they face many more months of drop cloths and plaster dust. Bill and I, though, are as happy as children at recess. Working on someone else's house turns out to be much more fun than working on your own: when you quit for the day, somebody else does the vacuuming. The other evening I finished my dinner in a hurry and hollered to my wife as I ran out the door, "Don't wait up for me! Billy and I are going over to Jimmy's house to play!"

# Spring Cleaning

**B**UYING TOYS FOR A CHILD warms your heart twice: first when you give them as gifts, then when you throw them away. Recently, I completed one of my semiannual search-and-destroy missions in the playroom. I filled ten thirty-gallon garbage bags with orphaned puzzle pieces, rock-hard lumps of Play-Doh, coverless comic books, Power Ranger torsos, party favors, Happy Meal prizes, mold-filled juice boxes, inch-long crayons, capless felt-tip markers, and several thousand other items that were either broken or hadn't been played with in more than a year (the statute of limitations for toy disposal). As I knotted the top of each newly filled garbage bag, I felt as jolly as Santa Claus on Christmas Eve. The only trick was to get all that loot out of the house before my kids got home from school. They never know where their own clothes are, but if you throw away a GI Joe flamethrower or one of Barbie's high heels, they sense the loss immediately and come hollering.

I have a friend who says she never walks through her children's rooms without throwing away a few Tinkertoys. That's a sound policy, but it doesn't eliminate the need for periodic full-scale rampages. Of course, neglected toys that are still in decent shape can be given to younger nephews, nieces, and others. But there's not much demand for Teenage Mutant Ninja Turtle arms. Even a seemingly simple toy can break down into dozens of useless components, the total volume of which greatly exceeds that of the original toy—a phenomenon that may account for the so-called "missing mass" that astrophysicists fret about.

The first time I cleaned up the playroom, I believed I was making a permanent improvement in my living environment. Even the kids seemed to appreciate the change, remarking that they hadn't realized the playroom had a rug. But of course everything was back to normal in a week or two. There's nothing a mere parent can do to halt the natural decomposition of a child's possessions. You might as well try to keep your hair from turning gray.

Grown-ups have a hard time managing their own belongings too, of course. When my wife and I moved to our house, our stuff—which had formerly fit into a one-bedroom apartment—mysteriously expanded to the point where we could barely squeeze it into a five-bedroom house. Being joggled inside a moving van apparently causes material possessions to expand. Before the movers had unloaded half their truck, we realized that we wouldn't be able to put everything away. We asked the movers to stack the extra boxes in the living room.

A law of physics states that a pile of boxes in a seldom used room will tend to remain there for a pretty long time. Sometimes that is good. A few years ago, my friends Rob and Marilyn moved from New York to Chicago. Two years later, they moved back. The second move was easier than the first, because roughly a quarter of their possessions were still sealed in packing boxes stacked on the living room floor. What had initially seemed like laziness on the part of Rob and Marilyn was revealed to have been careful planning.

Of course, in the end, the joke was on Rob and Marilyn. Their belongings, already swollen by the move to Chicago, mushroomed again during the move back to New York. Marilyn ended up having to give away Rob's fishing tackle, old *Playboy* magazines, and many of his golf shirts. They'll never be able to move again, unless they get rich or have a fire.

I'm better than my wife at throwing things away, but I do have some blind spots. Unfortunately, I inherited my father's inability to throw away any piece of paper that has a number printed on it. To get from the door of my office to my desk, I have to step inside several large cardboard boxes filled with canceled checks and credit-card statements. The only good thing about having a messy office is that you can always decide to spend the day cleaning it up instead of starting an important work project whose deadline is tomorrow.

My sister once lived in a house that had (she boasted) several thousand square feet of closet space. I felt envious until I saw the closets. They were big, all right, but you couldn't have squeezed a child's sock into any of them. My sister, inebriated by the thought of finally having enough storage space, had briefly stopped throwing things away. That was all the encouragement her possessions needed. By the time she realized what was happening, it was too late. Her stuff had already won.

# Finishing Up

S EVERAL YEARS AGO, I gutted an old bedroom on the third floor of my house and turned it into an office. I had someone else lay the carpet, but I did the rest of the work myself. I did the wiring and hung the wallboard, and I built the bookcases, cabinets, counters, and desk. Doing all that took up most of my spare time for most of a year, but it made me feel happy and fulfilled, and I ended up with an office that is pretty much exactly suited to the way I like to work. (I can see the TV from anywhere in the room; I can reach almost everything I need without standing up; if I lean back, I can see the UPS man in the driveway.)

The only thing I haven't been able to do in my office is to finish it. The doors on the cabinets remained unbuilt for five or six years when I gave up and hired someone else to build them, and they remained unpainted for several more. Once I finally did manage to make myself paint them—a job that took just a few hours spread over a long weekend—I needed six more months to buy knobs. And I still haven't painted the door to the office itself.

There are almost always a lot of unfinished projects around my house. When a newspaper reporter asked me, a few years ago, which home-improvement project I found most daunting, I said, "The last ten percent of anything I start." Down in the basement are some partitions that I have framed but never finished. In my wife's and my bedroom is a closet that for a full year didn't have a closet rod (or paint or hardware) and was thus unusable, except as a place to store the tools I had used the last time I worked on the closet. The baseboard in my daughter's room is still missing its shoe molding. One window in my son's room lacks one stop.

It is an axiom of home improvement that the final stages of any project consume slightly more than all the time and money. When my wife and I had a screened porch added to our house, the carpenters banged together the frame and roof in no time, then spent what seemed like several years hanging the screens and installing the interior trim. The simple explanation is that broad strokes go faster than finishing touches, but there are also psychological factors. Driving the final nail is difficult. Once it's in, there's nothing left to do but step back in judgment. As long as something remains undone, there's a chance that the next step, whatever it is, will pull everything together, creating a masterpiece.

One of the carpenters who built my porch told me that he likes to keep six or seven unfinished projects around his house, so that he'll have plenty of options whenever he decides to do a little work on his own time. His wife thinks he's too lazy to finish what he starts, but I don't think that's the real explanation. Each of those projects is like one of his children; finishing it would be the equivalent of sending it to college.

I *enjoyed* working on the closet in my bedroom. Once I started hanging clothes in it, though, it became just another closet, no different from any of the other closets in this house. But as long as I could still see bare Sheetrock, my closet belonged to me.

# SUMMER

# The Mind's Nose

THE MOST IMPORTANT PART of any summer house is its smell. Of course, there should also be sand on the floor. But all the really crucial features are olfactory: mothballs, mildewed paperback mystery novels, gin and limes, sea salt, very old dust, horsehair mattresses, last night's lobster leftovers, canvas seat covers, low-top sneakers not endorsed by athletes, and windblown, sun-scorched native vegetation. When you walk into a summer house that smells right, the first whiff transports you immediately to the best parts of your childhood. All the work-related sectors of your brain go dormant, and you begin to think that you might like to play a little Scrabble.

A summer house should not smell like your regular house. Even more important, it should not smell like someone else's regular house. There should be no air freshener. No lingering aroma of big wet dog. No dank, dandruffy shag carpet. No plumbing mysteries. No cleaning products advertised on TV. When you walk through the door, you should not immediately picture tubby people wearing dark socks with shorts and drinking off-brand beer while watching the Home Shopping Network.

Nor should a summer house smell like a motel room. Not that there's anything wrong with the way a motel room smells. In fact, the smell of a nice motel room is right up there with the smell of a new car. It's a modern, manufactured smell, but it has, for most people, sublime associations. The smell of a motel room makes you feel adventurous yet protected. It's mildly exotic, but it's also homey, in that it reminds you of every other motel room you've ever stayed in. It makes you want to turn on the TV and go down the hall for a bucket of ice. Still, it's not the right smell for a summer house.

Smells are powerful because the parts of our brains that interpret them are older than consciousness. There's a fragrant grove of pine and spruce trees behind my house. The first time I walked into it, I came as close as I have ever come to having an out-of-body experience. The grove smelled like a summer camp I went to when I was twelve. For a moment, I was overwhelmed by what I can describe only as a physical memory of that camp. I didn't simply recollect it—I was there. Now, years later, the effect is gone. The grove now smells only like the grove. Every time I walk into the trees, my brain overwrites its old scent files, and my memories of summer camp recede.

My wife, our kids, and I spend some time each summer at the same place on Martha's Vineyard. The house satisfies all my vacation-scent requirements. One of the most important smells comes from a boxwood hedge that runs under some of the windows. We have boxwood in our yard back at home, too, and I try to avoid smelling it, so that I won't take the edge off my summers. The continuity of the smells from summer to summer puts those vacations on a separate time line from the rest of my life. Each Vineyard vacation takes up where the previous one left off.

The smell of a summer house is potent because you smell it only once a year. You could increase its power by making the rest of your life smell even more different—perhaps by wearing a certain deodorant or aftershave lotion only during your vacation, or by eating a certain kind of food, or by wearing certain clothes, which you would keep during the rest of the year in an old trunk laced with mothballs. If you worked at it, you could erect an imperme-able fragrance barrier between your vacations and the rest of your life. One vacation would flow into the next. The intervening fifty weeks would evaporate like a half-remembered dream.

# Living with Ghosts

I LIVE FULL-TIME IN A PLACE where other people go on vacation. My town is about a two hours' drive north of Manhattan, and it is a source of second homes for New Yorkers of the lawyering-and-investment-banking class. It's the sort of mythical-seeming New England village where almost everyone recognizes almost everyone else's car, you don't need a ticket to pick up your snapshots or your dry cleaning, and people don't necessarily lock their doors when they go on vacation. (When we bought the place, I asked the previous owner for the key to the back door. He said he wasn't sure he had one, but that I wouldn't need it because the door didn't close all the way.) Living here, I have a feeling of mildly anxious contentment that I can only think to describe as self-envy.

Roughly two thousand of my town's four thousand residents show up only on weekends during nice weather and for occasional longer stretches during the summer. A few of the richest may appear on their sprawling estates for just a week or two in August, and they skip some years altogether. There's a famous musician down the road who spends less time in his house than the person who drops by to make sure his furnace hasn't melted down. I hear the musician's songs on the radio far more frequently than I see his car in his driveway.

Many of my town's full-time citizens feel a sort of moral

obligation to resent the part-timers, whom they refer to scornfully as "weekenders." In truth, there are grounds for resentment. The phantoms arrive in a wave of Volvos and Range Rovers
on Friday evenings and decamp before dinner on Sundays. They
don't care what anything costs. They view rainy weather as a personal affront. They don't know where anything is. They clog the
aisles of the grocery store on Saturday mornings. They don't
know the names of the people who work at the gas station, the
hardware store, the pizza place, or the bank. They view the
mediocre local lunch counter not as a mediocre local lunch
counter but as a quaint, cherished find.

Despite the weekenders' many failings, though, I like living
in a place where half the residents are ghosts. I try to think of the
part-timers not as an invading army but as a benevolent local
industry. They pump money into the town, often recklessly, but
they don't pump hazardous chemicals into the river. They enable
the rest of us to live in a place that looks like something we can't
afford. They pay local taxes but don't send their kids to local
schools. They do all their voting and five-sevenths of their toilet
flushing in New York. They dole out generous stipends to local
plumbers, waiters, cabinetmakers, caterers, the florist, real estate
agents, accountants, and storekeepers. Because of them, the grocery store carries arugula, shiitake mushrooms, and imported
beer. Some of my friends grumble about how crowded the store
is on Saturdays and Sundays, but if the weekenders were
replaced by people who lived here on weekdays, too, the grocery
store would be crowded all the time.

My feelings about the weekenders are tempered also by my
knowledge that I am a ghost, too. For a little while each summer,
my wife, our kids, and I leave home to intrude on the regular

lives of the full-time residents of Martha's Vineyard. There, we view rainy weather as a personal affront, clog the aisles of the grocery store on Saturday mornings, and help make parking places scarce. There, we are resentees rather than resenters.

The curious truth is that this sort of resentment is not entirely unpleasant, either on the giving or the receiving end. I'm sure that I appreciate my little town more because I know it is precious to the weekenders. And my own vacations seem more valuable to me when the full-timers on Martha's Vineyard look at me as though they think I'm robbing them. It is human nature to judge what one has in accordance with what others think of it. It is human nature to love what others want.

# Homes Away from Home

WHEN OUR DAUGHTER WAS not quite three, we took her to Disneyland. We worried that she might be too young, but we were staying in Los Angeles, and we couldn't think of anything else to do, so why not? When we asked her later what her favorite part of Disneyland had been, she said, "The horse." It turned out that she meant the coin-operated merry-go-round in front of a Kmart where we had stopped to buy diapers on our way to Anaheim.

You can never tell what's going to make an impression on a child. One of the few things I remember about the 1964 World's Fair, to which my parents took my sister and me when I was nine and she was six, was getting caught in the closing doors of a Manhattan subway train. I wasn't scared. I just had the vaguely happy feeling that I was going to be getting a lot of attention pretty soon. It was the same feeling I had had a year or two earlier, when, more or less on purpose, I had fallen through thin ice at the edge of a pond while skating.

Like virtually all the vacations I took as a child, that trip to the World's Fair was a car trip. Our home was in Kansas City, and getting to New York took two full days. I don't remember anything in particular about the drive, but I have fond memories of the car. It was a 1964 Buick Skylark station wagon, and it had a little window in the roof above the backseat. I do remember that my sister and I were excited about the prospect of looking at tops of skyscrapers through that roof window. The car also had brown vinyl seats on which it was easy to make lick lines. A lick line is a saliva boundary, drawn with your finger, that shows your sister how close to you she can move without being punched. (This was in the days before almost anyone wore seat belts, so trespassing was a problem.) Maintaining a lick line requires contributions from both parties, as in the famous poem about walls by Robert Frost.

Our car must have seemed practically empty during that trip, because we had left my one-and-a-half-year-old brother at home, with one of my grandmothers. The summer before, though, we had taken him with us to northern Michigan in a car that was smaller and didn't have air-conditioning. Also, a college-aged baby-sitter came with us. How did we survive? One year recently, my wife and I briefly considered taking both our cars on a two-hundred-fifty-mile trip to the beach, because we didn't see how we could possibly cram ourselves, our two kids, and all our stuff into just a minivan.

Even though I don't have many early memories of actual vacations, I have many vivid memories of motels. Once, when I was seven or eight, my sister and I talked our father into letting us try the vibrating bed in our motel room. He put in a quarter, and the bed began to shake. It also began to make a sound that was like the sound of a vacuum cleaner being fed slowly into a Cuisinart. The control box didn't have an off switch; it was wired directly into the wall and couldn't be unplugged. The bed either shook all night or seemed to shake all night, and my sister and I fought about whose turn it was to lie on it.

Despite the logistical difficulties, I like traveling with children. It forces you to do the things you really enjoy (buying souvenirs, going to Disneyland, eating at Wendy's) and to skip the things you really don't (going to plays, touring the wine country, looking at art). Keeping your kids from slitting each other's throats compels you to find activities that are actually interesting, as opposed to merely sounding like the kinds of activities that people engage in when they are on vacation.

Traveling with children also reminds you that you can find fun almost anywhere. Some of my happiest vacation memories involve a trip my family took with several other families when I was ten or eleven years old. We all stayed in a nice motel, went swimming, played miniature golf, and so on. The really great thing about the trip was that the motel was only ten miles away from where we all lived. Driving there took fifteen minutes. Nobody had to throw up or go to the bathroom, and nobody asked when we would be there. The kids had an entire motel to run around in, and the parents had plenty of time for cocktails. The next day, before lunch, we went home.

# Testing Owen's Law

OWEN'S LAW OF HOME IMPROVEMENT states, "The knowledge one gains in the course of doing something is the knowledge one ought to have had before trying it in the first place." In other words, learning by doing invariably means learning by doing wrong. I was reminded of this recently by a rabbit.

Every few weeks, my wife and children bring home a new pet. Sometimes, the new pet is a cat or a hamster. Not infrequently, it is an Israeli hedgehog or an African pygmy mouse. Most recently, it was a rabbit.

As soon as the rabbit arrived, I volunteered to build it a hutch. This seemingly generous offer was in fact entirely selfish. Without a hutch, I knew, the rabbit would live inside our house, which was already crowded with cages and aquariums. (The hedgehog sleeps on a heating pad, year-round, because it hibernates at room temperature.)

As luck would have it, a friend of mine had recently found himself in the same situation. His wife and children had come home one day with two rabbits, and he had offered to build a hutch in order to get them out of the house. My friend is in the awning business. He built the frame of his hutch out of the same kind of extruded aluminum that he uses to build the frames of awnings. The hutch even has a sliding aluminum tray in the bottom, suspended below the wire-mesh floor, to simplify cleaning.

Looking at that beautiful, complicated hutch, I felt jealous and inadequate. But then my friend made a confession. He said that the sliding aluminum tray—the hutch's most brilliant feature, in my view—had been a terrible mistake. He had made the tray slightly smaller than the floor of the cage, so that it would be easy to remove. The problem was that the rabbits invariably relieved themselves in the quarter-inch gap between the side of the cage and the edge of the tray. The tray, it turned out, made cage cleaning harder, not easier. My friend's wife and children viewed him not as a brilliant fabricator of extruded aluminum but as a home-improvement failure.

My friend's mistake was my good fortune, of course. By learning from someone else's experience, I would be able to cheat Owen's law. I went home and built a simpler but perfectly adequate hutch out of two-by-fours, plywood, and wire mesh. With my friend's experience fresh in my mind, I attached the mesh to the inside of the frame, and in such a way that the rabbit would not be able to make a mess of the two-by-fours. Instead, its droppings would fall harmlessly, and perhaps beneficially, into a bed of pachysandra below.

The next morning, I saw my wife in the backyard, cleaning the bottom of the hutch with a Dustbuster. "You don't need to do that," I said proudly. She said, "Yes, I do." I looked inside, then called my friend. "What size of wire mesh did you use on the bottom of your hutch?" I asked. "Half-inch," he said. I had used quarter. A typical rabbit dropping, it turns out, has a diameter of five-sixteenths of an inch.

The next night, the temperature briefly dropped below sixty degrees. All three rabbits moved indoors, and none has been outside since.

# The Futility of Home Improvement

THE APPALLING TRUTH ABOUT home improvement is that much of it is futile. You could spend a million dollars perking up your living room, yet at your next dinner party you would still find guests in the laundry room resting drinks on piles of folded underpants.

When my wife and I have company, we typically make a frantic last-ditch effort to gather domestic debris from the nice rooms and throw it into the playroom. Then the guests arrive, make a quick pass through the civilized parts of the house, and settle among the hamster cages.

My parents live in a nice house that they remodeled from the ground up. My mother's favorite part of it is the unfinished basement. She has a telephone, a TV, and an exercise machine down there, and she has a computer that sits on a table made from a sheet of plywood. The floor is bare concrete interrupted by the occasional carpet scrap. The decorating budget was perhaps four dollars. For my mother, though, the space is irresistible. She is drawn there by the same force that causes a child to be less interested in an expensive new toy than in the box it came in.

Like most people, I dream of having a kitchen that costs more than the rest of my house. I want granite counters and

Corian floor tiles and a refrigerator the size of a minivan. But my favorite kitchen on earth doesn't have any of those things. It's small and uncomfortable, and it's attached to one end of a barn on Martha's Vineyard. It doesn't have a bread machine or even a dishwasher. But it does have a yellow-pine counter that's fun to sit on, and just above the two-burner hot plate is a window through which you can watch the August sun go down.

Everyone in my house has a nice bedroom that was remodeled at considerable expense. But my kids' favorite place to sleep is a messy room that has a big, insulation-filled hole in the ceiling where a dormer used to be. It's not really a bedroom. It's a junk room in which one of the pieces of junk happens to be a bed. Sleeping there is more fun than sleeping in a room that looks as though it's meant for sleeping. Sleeping there would be even more fun if the bed were just a mattress on the floor.

Would my kids be happier if I tore holes in the ceilings of their rooms and filled their closets with boxes of ten-year-old tax records? Probably not. Nor would our dinner guests flock into our living room if we moved the washer and drier in there. A tattered old sweater wouldn't feel as comfortable if you didn't also own a three-piece suit. It's knowing that you have to go back to work on Monday that makes reading the Sunday paper so compelling.

For a similar reason, expensive home-improvement projects are probably worth the money after all. You may never use your fancy new living room, but if you didn't have it, your laundry room would be just a place to wash your clothes.

# Home Video

SOME TIME AGO, I became the last person in America to finally cave in and buy a video camera. I did not buy it for the usual reasons. I did not intend to use it to record birthday parties, school plays, or piano recitals. I was not planning to do what a woman sitting next to me on an airplane did, which was to shoot two or three minutes of tape out her window while the plane took off from Atlanta, put her camera away, boredly flip back and forth through Delta's in-flight magazine while humming nasally for more than an hour, eat only the cookie on her lunch tray, sleep for about twenty minutes with her mouth all the way open, take her camera back out, and shoot two or three minutes of tape out her window while the plane landed in Hartford.

I bought my camera for three reasons only: first, to make one of those videotaped inventories of my house and all my valuable possessions, so that my insurance company will cheerfully pay my claim in full when my house (but not the videotape) is destroyed; second, to record my golf swing in the hope of determining why I am such a crummy golfer; three, to provide occasional amusement to my children, whose sole criterion in judging human behavior is whether or not the behavior, if videotaped, would have a chance of being shown on *America's Funniest Home Videos*.

Why do people who lack such focused objectives buy video cameras? When my wife's sister got married, a neighbor videotaped the reception, as a wedding gift. My wife and her other sister grabbed the first cassette as soon as it was full, and several of us took it inside to watch it, even though the reception itself was still going on. Except for the parts featuring oneself, the tape was agonizingly dull. People who presumably had been saying interesting things stopped saying them as soon as the camera pointed at them, and began saying, "Don't you dare point that thing at me!" or "Testing, testing" or "I can't believe you're taping me eating a piece of liver!" or "Party time!" or "Hey, *Candid Camera*."

Do people actually watch the videotapes they make? A tape that takes two hours to make requires another two hours to watch, and no one whose life is worth taping has that much free time. Furthermore, a decision to record even a single event has mind-boggling implications. Once you have recorded your daughter's fourth birthday party, how can you justify not recording her fifth? Taping even a single event forces you indelibly to divide the moments of your life into two nonoverlapping categories: those that are worthy of subsequent viewing and those that are not.

The popularity of video cameras arises from a simple but potent misunderstanding. Somehow people have got the idea that they won't mind being old so much if they can turn on the TV and see what they were like when they were young. In fact, the opposite is true. The best memories—the ones that actually do comfort people in their later years—are ones that have been allowed to evolve unhindered by documentary proof. When I feel weary and infirm, I often cheer myself up by thinking back on my days as the star of my junior high school football team. These thrilling recollections would be less compelling if they were accompanied by a videotape, which would show that I weighed eighty pounds and spent most of my time on the bench. Memory is better than a video camera, because, in addition to being free, it doesn't work very well.

As for my own video camera, here's what I've done so far: I haven't made my inventory yet, because my house seems to be in no immediate danger of being destroyed; I have videotaped my golf swing, but the results were so depressing that I have not only given up taping my swing but very nearly given up golf; I have spent about ten minutes videotaping my children, who were interested at first but became bored as soon as they realized that nothing hilarious—such as a cat flushing a toilet or a fat man breaking a diving board—was likely to happen in our yard. Then I put my camera back in its case, and I haven't touched it since.

# The Bed Question

**M**Y KIDS DON'T MAKE THEIR beds every morning. In fact, they don't make them any morning. That's probably a good thing. If the kids did make their beds, my wife and I might feel guilty and discouraged, because we don't make ours.

Some readers, I'm certain, are already reaching angrily for their letter-to-the-author stationery. A decline in bed making, these readers will complain, ranks right up there with no-lick stamps as undeniable evidence that everything good in the world is being replaced by something bad.

I kind of believe that myself (except about the stamps). And yet, I'm torn. The classic argument in favor of requiring your children to make their beds—that they will grow up to be slobs if you don't—doesn't seem to hold in our case, since my wife and I both made our beds as children. We did it as adults, too—right up until the time we had kids. Over the years since then, we've gradually drifted toward my father's point of view (overruled by my mother), which is that bed making restricts sheet-to-blanket air flow and may, therefore, be harmful to a bed.

Maybe bed making skips generations. If that's the case, my wife and I are doing our kids a favor, by setting a bad example against which they will inevitably rebel. That means they'll become bed makers in early adulthood and never look back.

Their children will be the type who like salad, sit up straight, and speak politely to grown-ups. Such children, of course, always end up in prison, but until they do, they make a big impression on their parents' friends.

In addition to not making beds, the people in my house for the most part don't put away laundry. A small room attached to my wife's and my bedroom has evolved, in recent years, into a sort of communal clothing bank. There's a chair in the room that we treat like an ATM for underwear. When the kids get up in the morning, they stumble in and make withdrawals.

Central laundry storage has advantages—putting all the pants in one pile is, for the pants on the bottom, the next best thing to ironing—but I sometimes feel twinges of guilt. I precipitated a minor crisis one evening by suggesting that we put away at least our socks. That idea was treated as dangerous and irrational, and I responded by flying off the handle, and so on. It turns out that everyone else prefers the current system, in which we keep all our socks in a single basket, like fruit in a cafeteria. There are so many orphan socks in the basket that at any moment only about a third of the total supply is available for use. (The orphan socks are like the big piece of lettuce under the fruit salad that you aren't supposed to eat.) Life at our house would be simpler if we could all agree on a single color, style, and size.

Every so often, either my wife or I will decide that enough is enough and declare that from now on we're not going to live like hurricane victims. But our resolve seldom lasts longer than a day or two. After all, choosing clothes from a pile on a couch seems almost like shopping—an emotional plus—and who says a car isn't the best place to store dry cleaning?

# A Room of One's Own

**M**Y BROTHER'S WIFE, Mimi, has a younger sister, named Marie. When the girls were seven and five, their family moved to a new house. Like most younger siblings, Marie was used to (and tired of) living on rejects and hand-me-downs. Her parents were sympathetic, and when it came time to assign bedrooms in the new house, they told Marie that for once she could choose first. Without hesitation, she said, "I want Mimi's room."

Grown-ups can leave their mark on the world in all sorts of impressive ways—skyscrapers, bank mergers, nuclear war—but a kid's sphere of influence is limited. Using a few crumpled scraps of duct tape to crookedly hang a Kurt Cobain poster on top of that expensive but outgrown nursery wallpaper is an early (and healthy) expression of contempt for local authority. Taking control of one's walls is a first step toward taking control of one's life.

When I was growing up, the room I envied most was that of my friend Ralph Lewis, who was allowed (or, at any rate, was not explicitly forbidden) to throw darts at the back of his door and conduct chemistry experiments on his floor. His principal field of research in those days was finding the melting points of various possessions. I still have a small scar on my arm that was made by a dollop of molten GI Joe. But the damage to my arm was trivial in comparison with what we did to the floor.

My own room was embarrassingly unimaginative. I made my only serious decorative statement in junior high school, when I hung my unrolled sleeping bag from the picture molding so that the down filling would not become compacted. The sleeping bag was expensive, and I had bought it with my own money. Hanging it on the wall was a reminder to my parents that I was just passing through. At any moment, I wanted them to know, I might head for the hills of Colorado, Alaska, Tibet, or some other place where their word was not the law.

My wife was a far more ambitious decorator. In 1968, when she was twelve, she persuaded her parents to provide her with surroundings worthy of the decade. At her direction, they installed black Kodel wall-to-wall carpeting and black-and-white zebra-striped vinyl wallpaper. (The white stripes were smooth and shiny; the black stripes were flock.) They covered one of her twin beds with a black corduroy spread from Sears, and the other with a white one. They trimmed the beds with throw pillows covered in black, white, and orange vinyl. They bought a butterfly chair with an orange canvas seat. They let her paint her dresser black. At dinnertime, she would retreat to her sanctuary, put on a prized pair of brown vinyl pants that she wasn't allowed to wear in public, and make angry entries in her diary.

My kids periodically decide that they would like to make similarly ambitious alterations in their own living quarters. I'm sympathetic to the impulse but reluctant to make big changes based on trends of the moment. After all, I know how my wife's decorating story turned out. A year after going black-and-white, she decided she preferred a colonial look, and her parents—outwardly upset about all that wasted plastic but inwardly relieved—helped her pull down the zebra stripes.

# Other People's Stuff

DURING ONE OF MY PERIODIC adrenaline-aided house-keeping frenzies, I hauled several tons of junk from my basement to my driveway. I called the guy who picks up my trash, and he agreed to stop by the next day. The pile stretched all the way from the basketball goal to the edge of the yard. It contained lumber scraps, old chairs, broken toys, broken tools, a rocking horse with rusted springs, some two-thirds-empty buckets of joint compound, and a cracked sink.

That afternoon, a man who was painting the front of my house knocked at the door and asked if he could have the chairs. A little later, the man who cuts my grass asked for the cracked sink and the joint compound. My son carried off most of the lumber scraps for a fort in the backyard. My daughter spotted the rocking horse, which had been her favorite possession ten years before, and screamed. I helped her carry it back to the basement. By the time the trash truck arrived, the pile was so small it scarcely warranted an extra trip to the dump.

No department store window ever tantalized passersby like a pile of junk in a driveway. If I had been more clever, I could have put price tags on several of the better items and recouped the cost of the trash pickup. I once bought a few books at an estate sale where the merchandise included old girdles and panty hose. And they weren't cheap, either.

Two friends once planned a yard sale and invited me to join them. I didn't have much to sell, but I did contribute two broken portable heaters and a broken vacuum cleaner, all three of which I labeled as broken. They sold immediately. I also unloaded some pants I had outgrown, some barbells I hadn't used since high school—if then—and a box of old magazines.

Of course, I bought as well as sold, and at the end of the day I went home with nearly as much stuff as I had come with. My two friends bought quite a bit, too. Indeed, if the three of us had pooled our purchases, we would have had more than enough inventory for yet another yard sale. That's probably what we ought to have done, since most yard sale bargains lose their allure as soon as you get them home.

Instead of holding yard sales, people ought to simply keep their junk in their yards. If you were walking your dog and spotted something interesting in a neighbor's pile, you could drive over later and load it into the back of your minivan, no charge. And as soon as you got tired of it—later that evening, let's say—you could toss it out your front door and put it back into circulation.

# Keeping Cool

ONE OF THE GREAT MYSTERIES of human evolution is why people seem to feel truly happy about the weather only four or five days a year. My personal comfort zone—which I have measured scientifically over a period of years by checking my pulse and respiration each morning as I step out my back door to pick up my newspaper while wearing only gym shorts and a T-shirt—seems to be about three degrees wide. When the temperature dips below that narrow band, I feel chilly; when it nudges above, I feel like lying on the basement floor. This exquisite sensitivity to heat and cold seems recklessly inefficient, from a survival point of view. Why did natural selection abandon human fur?

Some people are more sensitive than others to changes in temperature. My mother can be chilled to the verge of hypothermia by a single briskly moving oxygen molecule. In that way, at least, she has a lot in common with our dachshund, who during the winter likes to lie on her side in front of a baseboard heating register in the library, with one foot pressed against each corner of the vent. The blast is so fierce that she has to hold her chin up to keep her eyes from drying out. Every hour or so she'll stagger into the kitchen for a drink of water, then stagger back to the vent. My daughter, in contrast, will occasionally walk out into the snow to feed the cats without bothering to put on shoes. Like the cats, who live outside year-round, she doesn't seem to notice the cold until the mercury drops well below zero.

Actually, cold doesn't bother me as much as heat. When you're cold, you can put on another sweater, run up and down the stairs, or curl up next to the dog on the library floor. But when you're hot, your options are limited.

I think about heat fairly often during the summer. My house is old, and it doesn't have central air-conditioning. Keeping it tolerably cool during the hottest parts of .he season is hard. But it's not impossible, as my wife and I have discovered. I now realize that air-conditioning has made people lazy and unimaginative when it comes to maintaining our tiny comfort zones.

People used to know more about keeping cool than they do now. My grandparents lived without air-conditioning in a hot part of the country, but they still managed to survive virtually a century apiece—and even in August my grandfather never took off his tie. They had awnings over their windows and venetian blinds behind their curtains, and they had a big basement fan that looked like a propeller salvaged from the *Titanic*. When I spent the night at their house during the summer, I would sleep on top of my covers with my head by the open window at the foot of my bed, and the basement zephyr would carry me off to sleep. I liked lying with my head by the window, because that way I could directly observe the many personal problems of my grandparents' neighbors, a large dysfunctional family.

At my own house, we don't have a basement fan, but we still manage to stay comfortable most of the summer. We have borrowed a trick from my wife's parents, who cool their own unair-conditioned house by opening most of their windows at night and then closing all the windows and most of the curtains during the day. Even a poorly insulated house, like mine, will stay fairly cool well into the afternoon if it's buttoned up tight before the temperature starts to climb. Last summer I bought a portable fan that fits snugly inside the opening of a second-floor window. I turn it on when I go to bed, and it cools the house so thoroughly that by early morning I often find myself groping for a blanket.

Living behind drawn curtains during the day can seem a little gloomy at times, but in compensation you feel less guilty about squandering fossil fuels. Best of all, the nosy people next door can't tell when you're having a fight.

# Children and Money

WHEN OUR SON WAS BORN, my wife and I needed a baby blanket for his crib. Our daughter, who was three and a half, had several old ones in her closet.

"What are you doing in my closet?" she demanded.

"Just getting one of these old blankets," my wife said.

"Why?"

"To give it to your new baby brother."

"I want it!" our daughter screamed.

"But, honey," I said, "you didn't even know that old blanket was there."

"I need it!"

"It's a *baby* blanket. Don't you want to give it to a baby?"

"I want it!"

My wife and I looked at each other in despair. What to do? Suddenly, my wife had an inspiration.

"Would you take five bucks for it?" she asked our daughter.

(No more crying.) "Okay."

Money is a handy tool if you use it properly. That's a lesson that most people don't learn until they've taken out a bigger mortgage than they can afford and hit the max on all their credit cards. In the hope of one day sparing my children that rude awakening, I brooded for a long time about how to teach them to take responsibility for their own financial affairs.

Parents seldom succeed in this area, because the arguments they use are weak. They tell their children, for example, that they should put some money away for a rainy day, and that a savings account—in just one year—will magically turn twenty-five dollars into twenty-five dollars *and seventy-five cents*. The problem, of course, is that to a kid a year is a thousand years long, and even to a grown-up a savings-account interest rate seems like a joke.

So, here's what I did: I started my own bank—called the First National Bank of Dave—and, using financial software that I use to keep track of my own checks, I opened an account for each of my children. Their allowances are deposited automatically on the first of each month and they can withdraw or deposit money any-time they want to. Here's the kicker: I told them I would pay them interest on their balances at a rate of five percent per month. That's right—per month. It works out to an annual rate of more than seventy percent. "If you save some money instead of spending it all," I told them, "in a little while, you'll be able to double or even triple your allowance."

Both kids instantly grasped the idea. (My son searched our cars and all our furniture for change, turning up several dollars' worth for immediate deposit.) Overnight, my children stopped being profligate squanderers and turned into calculating savers. In fact, their balances quickly grew so high that after a couple of years I had to roll back the monthly interest rate to three percent, a change that gave me an opportunity to explain the inexorable law of supply and demand.

The money in the First National Bank of Dave belongs to the depositors, no strings attached. If they want to spend it on some-thing I think is dumb, that's their business. To reinforce that sense of responsibility, I try to make sure that every penny they spend passes through the bank first. If we're about to go on vacation, I'll add twenty or thirty dollars to each account and tell my kids that they can spend the extra money on souvenirs, or keep it, or do anything with it they like—even spend it now—but that I won't give them any more money during the trip.

The key to teaching children a long-term perspective on saving is to give them a short-term incentive for doing it. My son used to spend every penny the moment it came into his hands, and why not? Shortly after I started m, bank, though, he told me that he liked to let his money "charge up" before spending it. To my kids, saving now seems like a reward, not a punishment. Instead of needling my wife and me to throw away money on stuff they don't really want, they coldly assess how much each potential purchase would cost them in foregone earnings—and, as often as not, they turn their backs and walk away.

# Designing Men

IN MOST CONVENTIONAL FAMILIES, the wife plays a larger role than the husband in home decoration. That probably explains why master bedrooms tend to contain many pretty chintz-covered-pillow-type items and not many soundproof riflery stalls. Most men are content with this state of affairs, figuring that the simplicity of doing nothing outweighs any possible advantages of getting involved. They buy themselves a vibrating leather recliner and an eighty-inch TV and let it go at that. But our homes might be very different if the men were in control.

In my own case, I know that if I were calling all the shots, my house would be far better suited to indoor sports than it is now. My model in this regard is my brother's old apartment in Brooklyn. His bedroom had a high ceiling and a large closet with mirror-covered folding doors. The bedroom was so large and the ceiling so high that he could stand in front of the mirrors and take full swings with a driver—something that I can't do without damaging the club on the relatively low ceilings of my house. In addition, my brother could arrange his closet doors so that he could see the same view of himself that an observer standing in front of him would see, rather than a mirror-reversed simulation. Best of all, my brother's wife thought of the mirrors not as a swing-training device but as a fashion aid and room brightener. The big mirrored doors—which serendipitously were already in the apartment when they bought it—were important to both of them, thus strengthening their marriage.

Had the ceilings in their apartment been just a few feet taller, my brother could have hung a hoop over the closet, pulled up the wall-to-wall carpeting, and hosted short-court basketball games with neighborhood friends on afternoons when it was too rainy to play outside. The mirrored doors would have provided the same opportunities for self-contemplation as the Jumbotrons in big football stadiums: You would have been able to watch yourself knifing past befuddled defenders for that game-winning last-second layup.

Of course, twenty-foot ceilings are hard to come by, even in those grand old mansions that nobody can afford anymore. In new construction, though, you can achieve reasonably useful room height without increasing the overall size of the house, by placing the master bedroom on the ground floor and the children's bedrooms directly above. By borrowing a little air space from the kids, you end up with a twelve-foot ceiling for yourself and a four-foot ceiling for them—a win-win situation, since kids love cozy, cavelike spaces and often don't surpass four feet in height until they're well into grade school.

To tell you the truth, I would be afraid to suggest such a decorating scheme to my wife. She's pretty traditional when it comes to things like having to crawl into your children's rooms to tuck them in at night. But I suspect that there are other areas in which she could be persuaded. For example, wouldn't it make sense to cover all our floors with that heavy black rubber stuff you sometimes see at little kids' playgrounds? That way you could wear your golf shoes right into the house.

# Nuts About Bathrooms

I N ATLANTA ONCE, I VISITED a show house that had been designed and built in connection with the annual trade show of the National Association of Home Builders. The master bathroom covered substantially more area than the master bedroom. It also opened onto a small courtyard (on the front of the house) in which, according to a brochure, the house's owners could "test the weather" before dressing. Upstairs was a double bathroom that had glass-block walls and a shower with clear glass doors. (No need to knock! You can see if it's occupied!)

Bathroom nuttiness isn't confined to show houses. When my friends Ken and Gina built their own house, shortly after getting married, they designed the master bedroom and bathroom as a single room. The sink, toilet, whirlpool bath, and shower were just a step up from the bed, with no door or wall or even curtain to set them apart. In theory, this arrangement promoted openness and intimacy. In practice, it made the bedroom look like a bathroom with a bed in it. Ken and Gina soon found that they preferred to use a different bathroom, which was down the hall and had a door. More recently, they abandoned their original idea altogether and built a new room to sleep in.

Ken and Gina's old bedroom/bathroom was a bit extreme, but it nonetheless embodied a number of peculiarly American trends in bathroom design, among them ostentation and exhibitionism. For quite a while now, big, fancy bathrooms have been viewed as necessities in high-end construction. They have also become status symbols. Twenty years ago, you wouldn't have been invited to take a guided tour of someone's $250,000 bathroom, as I was recently (fireplace, three sinks, exercise equipment, picture window next to the pond-sized tub). Now, though, you would. I haven't heard of anyone hiring a full-time attendant to flush the toilet and hand out towels, but I probably just move in the wrong crowd.

A few years ago my parents sold the big old suburban house in which I grew up. It was built in the twenties, and it had a sort of master-bedroom suite consisting of a semi-enormous sitting room and a somewhat smaller bedroom (known in the days before air-conditioning as a sleeping porch). The bathroom, which opened off the sitting room, was merely normal-sized, with no space for a Jacuzzi. Many potential buyers viewed this arrangement as hopelessly archaic, and, partly as a result, the house stayed on the market for more than a year. The increasingly nervous real estate agent suggested to several prospects that the place could be salvaged by turning the bedroom into a bathroom and the sitting room into a bedroom, an operation that had already been performed on a few other houses in my parents' neighborhood.

That anyone would trade living space for tooth-brushing space seems strange to me. In my own dream house, the bathrooms would be small and made entirely of plastic, so they could be hosed down. There would be room for magazines, but there would be no fireplace, and I would leave the exercise equipment in the basement, where it wouldn't be underfoot during those times (always) when it wasn't being used.

# The Next Big Thing

I ONCE ASKED A GOLF-CLUB MANUFACTURER why the heads of his golf clubs were made of a particular exotic alloy. He said, "Some golfers feel more confident looking down at a more expensive club." A similar notion explains various aspects of the higher end of the kitchen-and-bathroom market. Some people simply feel better about themselves while sitting on toilets that have gold flecks baked into their finishes.

When my sister got married, a friend gave her a charcoal grill and an end table. The only connection between the grill and the table was that the grill by itself hadn't cost quite enough. Anyone who has shopped for wedding presents understands this predicament. The gift that seems perfect for the bride and groom invariably turns out to cost two thirds of what you figure a self-respecting wedding guest ought to spend, and the clerk refuses to raise the price, so you have to either buy something else or throw in an end table.

This same quirk of human nature explains kitchen counters made of marble. If marble were cheap, no one would use it for kitchen counters. It's absurdly heavy, it stains easily, it absorbs water, it's nearly impossible for contractors to work with, and it's lethal to thin-stemmed wineglasses. It can also make a kitchen look like the men's room in a nineteenth-century train station. But it costs a fortune and, as a result, is comforting to a certain type of person—perhaps even to oneself. As a matter of fact, I wouldn't mind having marble counters in my own kitchen. But then, I don't do much cooking.

Kitchens and bathrooms haven't always been the objects of materialistic longing. Not so long ago, kitchens and bathrooms were just kitchens and bathrooms. For June Cleaver, remodeling the kitchen meant buying new curtains, and who cared about bathrooms? Curiously, the fantasy value of kitchens has risen as their practical value has declined. You don't need marble counters and a professional-model range to thaw a plastic pouch of low-fat lasagna. Most of the cooking that most people do nowadays could be done just as easily with a single burner and a microwave. In fact, you could probably do it in a bathroom.

For some time, I've wondered what the next major home-improvement fad will be. Fancy kitchens and bathrooms have been hot since at least Ronald Reagan's first term. The main reason they get so much attention is that they are the easiest parts of a house to make more expensive. But tastes invariably change, and remodelers will eventually have to turn their attention somewhere else. Where?

How about the garage? The idea sounds implausible, I realize. What could be more mundane than a garage? But forty years ago, no one would have believed that a certain type of American would someday feel inadequately sheltered in any house whose principal bathroom lacked a fireplace and a wet bar. Ten or twenty years from now, people with money on their hands may feel the same way about parking their cars on anything less than Mexican tile. How about extra bays for entertaining? A fireplace, of course. And floor-to-ceiling windows, so the neighbors can look in.

# Walls Within Walls

FUSSING WITH SOME CRUMBLING PLASTER in my dining room once, I glimpsed a bit of wallpaper in the cavity behind the studs. I chipped away more plaster and aimed a flashlight into the darkness. Six inches behind the visible wall was another plaster wall, perhaps an original one. The wallpaper on the older wall was every bit as ugly as any wallpaper you can buy today, and beneath it there was other wallpaper, and beneath that there was thick, peeling paint. The older plaster was cracked, but it was still cold and smooth. The lath in the older wall had been hand-split, and the nails handmade. The bottom third of the wall was missing. Some nineteenth-century owner must have removed the original raised-panel wainscot and put it some-where else—perhaps in my living room, where paneling conceals another forgotten wall.

Almost any house that has reached a certain age contains other houses. Some are virtually intact. Some are no thicker than a sheet of wallpaper or a coat of latex paint. Over the years, my wife and I have added a few layers of our own. We dealt with the broken plaster in the dining room and living room by covering it with Sheetrock—layers upon layers upon layers. We have also removed layers. Under the wallpaper in our daughter's room we discovered adolescent graffiti from a mysterious ancient era—1969, when Richard Nixon was president and the house was a boarding-school dormitory. In the room that became my office, I stripped the walls down to the studs and discovered mouse nests that may be almost as old as the nation. Under the attic floor I found a scrap of old pine with a pair of copperplate signatures on it: Leonard Agard and F. W. Richmond. The names of two eighteenth-century builders? I thought so, until I found Leonard Agard in the phone book. He's still installing floors.

At the place we visit every summer on Martha's Vineyard,* the oldest parts of the house date from the late 1600s, but so many hands have worked there that you can't tell which parts came when. One recent fall, a pair of carpenters undertook to deal with some long-neglected walls, ceilings, rotting sills, joists, and floorboards. Under the floor in the main hallway the carpenters found another floor, and under that floor they found another. A couple of hundred years ago, apparently, the original joists had rotted and the original floor had collapsed, and some ancient builder simply laid a new floor on top of the old one. Sometime later, that floor collapsed, too, and another layer was added. The bottommost floor was resting on a few irregular stones on the bare ground. Near the stairway was a rectangular arrangement

---

* Our Vineyard place is almost impossible to categorize. It's an old farm, which a small group of skinny-dipping Easterners bought for a pittance in 1917. They placed the property in a trust, and the trust today exists for the benefit of roughly twenty member couples, of which my wife and I are one. The farm covers forty acres near the ocean and includes an old house, a renovated eighteenth-century barn, a pair of chicken coops that have been converted into minimal living quarters, and seven rustic cabins. The number of people in residence at any moment ranges between none and about thirty. Every summer, the group hires a cook and two chore people, and we eat our meals together in the barn. As has been true since the earliest days, members and their guests spend an hour and a half after breakfast painting, pruning, and otherwise maintaining the property. An older member once called the place "the only successful communist society in the world."

of stones that may have represented the footprint of the original house, which had long since been absorbed into the dwelling that grew around it. The walls turned out to be four walls thick, each one separately framed, and there were two ceilings. The house itself had little structure, the carpenters told me—just a minimal timber frame covered with rough sheathing. The oldest plaster had been spread directly on the backs of the sheathing boards, which had been scored with an ax. For a couple of centuries, the house had been held up mainly by the abandoned houses inside it. Before framing the new floor, the carpenters hauled out twenty tons of rotten sills, rotten joists, rotten floorboards, dirt, and stones.

We felt a little guilty about sending all those abandoned houses to the dump—but not too guilty. If the original builders had had concrete and pressure-treated lumber, they would have used them, too. Besides, when the carpenters were finished, the house looked pretty much exactly the way it had before they began. The place is some forty thousand pounds lighter, but the parts you can see look the same as the parts they replaced. We didn't make any truly radical changes. We just took the next logical step in a continuous process that has been going on for more than three hundred years.

# Bathrooms and America

THE FIRST TIME I SAW A BIDET, in a hotel room in Paris, I mistook it for something else. I had a feeling I was missing the point (why hot and cold taps?). But the bathroom was way down at the other end of the hall, and I was twenty years old and having an adventure. Besides, that bidet was by no means the strangest piece of plumbing I encountered in Europe.

Nothing seems more foreign than a foreign bathroom. Even in allegedly developed countries, a toilet is sometimes just a hole in the floor, and the toilet paper is hard and shiny, like wax paper, and seems to have been impregnated with insecticide.

Not long ago, I spent a week in Scotland. British bathrooms are considerably less horrifying than French or Italian ones, but they are still sufficiently different from American bathrooms to make me glad I live in the most wasteful country on earth. Still, some good came of the trip. My exposure to Scottish bathrooms, though brief, enabled me to see the bathrooms of my homeland in a new light, and I had two ideas about how American bathrooms might be improved.

First, we should return to the rubber plug. In virtually all modern American bathrooms, the sinks and tubs employ complex mechanical systems to prevent water from running down the drain. All three bathtubs in my house have trip-lever drains, each of which consists of a heavy brass plunger suspended inside the waste pipe by a series of metal rods and threaded yokes, and controlled by a chrome-plated lever mounted in the middle of the chrome-plated overflow plate. When you pull the lever up, the plunger drops into the waste line and blocks it; when you push the lever down, the plunger rises an inch or two into the overflow pipe, permitting water from the tub to run out. The bathroom sinks in my house all have pop-up stoppers, which are controlled by similarly elaborate assemblages of rods, levers, and springs. All of these devices are balky and unreliable. All require periodic adjustment. All have a tendency to become encrusted with toothpaste, hair, and tub slime. Replacing any of them would cost real money and would require the skills of either a plumber or a semi-ambitious do-it-yourselfer. In contrast, rubber plugs—which are ubiquitous abroad—are basically foolproof. You could buy a hundred of them for less than the price of a single trip-lever drain.

Second, the ideal place to install a shower is in a bathtub. In recent years, there has been a trend in upscale American bathroom design to maintain a distinct division between bathing and showering. Wealthy Americans, apparently, feel poor if forced to stand where others have sat, or vice versa. In almost any fancy American bathroom nowadays, the tub is enormous and is mounted on a platform in front of a picture window, and the shower is enormous and is situated across the room inside a large, clear-glass enclosure. This arrangement necessitates a lot of redundant plumbing and waterproofing. It also ignores the fact that the average bathtub, being large and deep, makes a better shower base than the average shower base, because it keeps water from slopping onto the floor.

Other than that, though, American bathrooms are better than foreign bathrooms. Maybe the best advice for an international traveler is to go before you leave.

# Deck Mania

I F A BOEING 747 EVER runs out of fuel above my house, the pilot will be able to make an emergency landing on my neighbor's deck, which is big enough to handle the late-afternoon traffic at La Guardia. My neighbor started with a small deck several years ago. He liked it so much that he tripled its size, then built two extensions at different elevations. The finished structure dwarfs the house, which now looks like a white cork bobbing in a pale-green sea.

Home-improvement projects can be divided into two categories: those that can be done, and those that should be done. Do-it-yourselfers tend to favor the former. For example, the ceramic-tile tub enclosure in the principal bathroom in my house began to seem unacceptably dilapidated shortly after we moved in. Some of the tiles were so loose I could have peeled them away with my fingers. But I didn't know anything about tiling in those days, so I decided instead to cover the deteriorated area with duct tape. I used half a roll, overlapping the strips horizontally, like clapboards. I figured the tape would last a couple of months, giving me time to conquer my fear of grout. (Instead, the tape lasted seven years, at which point I capitulated and hired a professional to do the job right.)

Building a great big pale-green deck is usually a job that can, as opposed to should, be done. Nailing together several thousand board feet of poison-impregnated yellow pine is easy—so easy, in fact, that many amateur home improvers have difficulty making themselves stop. If one deck is good, then two must be better. Another neighbor of mine has now added a deck to virtually every room in his house. Two of the larger decks are connected by a smaller deck. If he could figure out a way to put decks on his decks, he would do it.

A really big deck is a little bit like a really big kitchen. The extra space sounds tempting in theory, but would your life really be any easier if your oven and your refrigerator were thirty feet apart? One summer, my neighbor with the pressure-treated runway threw an outdoor cocktail party. Most of the guests crammed together like cockroaches in one tiny corner of his masterpiece. On a square-footage basis, my friend did not get his money's worth out of his deck that night.

My own preference in outdoor sitting areas is for old-fashioned screened porches of relatively modest size. As it happens, my house has such a porch. My wife and I had it built several years ago to replace a rotting porch that was too small to use. Our new porch measures roughly fifteen feet by fifteen feet. It has a floor made of quarter-sawn tongue-and-groove fir, which I stained slightly darker than its natural color. Because it has screens, the bugs don't eat us up. Because there is a roof above it, the furniture looks pretty much like normal furniture, and we can sit out there when it's raining. We spend a lot of time on that porch during the warm months—a lot more time than we would spend on a deck. And we don't have to watch out for airplanes.

# Life Behind Screens

YOU CAN TELL A LOT ABOUT the self-confidence of do-it-yourselfers by watching what they do immediately after being awakened in the middle of the night by the smell of burning electrical insulation. I—this anecdote is autobiographical—ran straight to my third-floor office, which is the only part of my house that I wired myself. While my wife and children continued to sleep peacefully one floor below, I got down on my hands and knees and frantically sniffed wall receptacles.

As it turned out, my Romex wasn't on fire. The smell that had awakened me was coming from the crawl space under our screened porch, where our cats had cornered a skunk. There's a big difference between the smell of a dead skunk flattened on a highway and the smell of a live skunk cornered under your porch. A live skunk cornered under your porch smells like burning electrical insulation.

The cats eventually decided to let the skunk go back to eating our garbage, but the smell was so bad that the porch remained off-limits for days. I hated waiting. During the warm months of the year that porch is pretty much my favorite part of our house.

I like to sit on my porch at night, after my children have gone to bed. I drink fake beer and read the newspaper and listen to moths the size of hummingbirds thudding into the screens. A good screened porch is sort of like a room, and sort of not. The screens let most of the outside in without letting much of the inside out. I can hear the frogs in the creek at the bottom of the hill, and I can smell various types of vegetation around the edges of the yard, but I don't feel entirely exposed, as I would if I were standing in my driveway. I probably would never walk around in my driveway wearing just my underpants, but I might do that in my porch.

I don't like big old screenless porches. Their edges are too blurry; there's no sense of enclosure. Turn on a lamp to read by, and the light seems to leak all over the neighborhood. Also, of course, the hummingbird-sized moths thud into you instead of into the screens, and you have trouble hearing the frogs over the whine of the mosquitoes circling your ears. The same thing happens on pressure-treated decks, which I also don't like. A deck is more nearly part of the yard than part of the house. There isn't enough difference between it and the pile of lumber from which it was built.

People will sometimes ruin a nice screened porch by enclosing it with sliding glass panels. They figure that the panels will enable them to use the porch during months when they otherwise wouldn't. Sometimes they'll even install an air conditioner. These people are missing the point. A porch with big glass panels isn't a porch anymore; it's a solarium, or worse. And a porch with an air conditioner is nothing at all.

If you live in a part of the country that has seasons, your porch should have seasons, too. When it's too cold to stand in your driveway, it should be too cold to stand in your porch. And when it's so hot that all you really want to do is stand in front of an open refrigerator, you should be able to go out on your porch with your fake beer and your sports section and think, "Oh, my God. *What* is that smell?"

# Let There Be Weeds

AN ARTICLE IN *THE NEW YORK TIMES* said that Americans spend more than $22 billion a year on their lawns. I am unashamed to admit that almost none of that money is spent by me. Of all the vices of encroaching middle age, caring about the yard is one that I have managed to avoid.

Not that our yard looks terrible. A guy with a truck full of noisy machines comes once a week to cut the grass and beat back the poison ivy. I haven't pulled down the value of my neighbors' property far enough to make lawsuits worth the bother. But if you get close to our lawn, you can see that the grass looks suspiciously like the stuff at the far end of the produce counter. It isn't turf, exactly. It's more like bok choy.

I didn't inherit my apathy from my parents. Both of them spent many hours in our yard while I was growing up, and we had flowers and tomatoes and weedless grass. My wife's parents are also blameless. In fact, local garden tours often feature their perennials. My father-in-law, after a hard week at work, thinks nothing of spending a hard weekend stirring coffee grounds into his compost heap. He has a greenhouse, and he knows the names of the plants he grows. Visiting our house gives him many opportunities to bite his tongue.

Luckily for me, we live in the country, where yards are judged by a lower standard than in the suburbs. We have friends with decent gardens, to be sure, but we also have friends who, like me, view dandelions as free chrysanthemums. Folks around here don't even water their grass, a fact that appalled my wife when we first moved in. Her father's example is a heavy burden for her. Not gardening, in her view, is the rough equivalent of not educating your kids.

The only time I managed to work up any enthusiasm for yard work was during a brief period when I owned a chain saw. Making a lot of noise and causing big things to fall over—that was something I could understand. But then I misjudged the lean of a dead red pine, and it fell toward both my house and the more expensive end of my saw. The house survived, but the saw did not, and my enthusiasm for lumberjacking died.

For a while we also owned a lawn mower. Like the chain saw, it was attractively noisy and destructive. But the trouble with mowing your own lawn, like the trouble with paying taxes, is that you can't wait to do it till inspiration strikes you. I might have felt different if I had owned a riding mower. I have friends who have fancy lawn tractors and profess to love them. Still, I suspect that what they really love is not the machine but the privacy it affords. The back of a riding mower may be the last place in America where you can't receive a telephone call.

There may be more to it than that, but if there is, I don't want to know. The appeal of lawn care, like the appeal of fly-fishing, is something I'm content not to understand.

# Insulation

I n 1989, the Rolling Stones spent the summer in my town. They needed a place to practice for a tour, so they paid about three hundred thousand dollars to rent three houses, a closed inn, and a defunct girls' boarding school. The closed inn, where the technicians and security guards stayed, was just down the road from my house. (The inn has since reopened.)

A few days before the band arrived, a delivery truck from a linen service pulled into my driveway. The driver said he was looking for the inn. Inside the truck were crisply folded sheets and pillowcases that pretty soon would be slept on by guys working for the Rolling Stones. To the driver of the truck, though, it was just another delivery. "I don't care whether this linen order is for the president of the United States or Joe Blow," his demeanor and expression seemed to say. "I'm going to deliver it (eventually) just the same." Admiring his professionalism, I gave him accurate directions to the inn.

Shortly before the Stones arrived, the nearest local newspaper—my town is too small to have its own—fretted that the band's presence might create a "circus" and that my town was now in danger of being overrun by "groupies, paparazzi, television crews, and the just plain curious—all causing more traffic and who knows what other kinds of headaches." The following week, someone I know wrote a letter to the editor defending the

Stones and referring to them as "these middle-aged profession-als." As it turned out, there wasn't much of a circus. Mick Jagger did spend a thousand dollars on wine at the liquor store, but he didn't drink it all himself. It was for his forty-sixth birthday party.

One person who was not impressed by the proximity of the Rolling Stones was my daughter, who was five. Her taste in music in those days ran more in the direction of Raffi. She referred to the music on MTV as "grown-up music." When she would hear grown-up music playing on the car radio she would ask for the car radio to be turned off. One day she told me she would like to have a Rolling Stones tape. She said it in the same way that I once said I would like to see what her Barbie shoes would look like if they were all lined up. That is, she didn't mean it.

One of my fantasies that summer was that I would run into a Rolling Stone while taking a walk and that we would fall into an easy, natural discussion of our children: their soccer teams, soft-ware preferences, television-viewing restrictions, and so forth. Then I was going to say, "Hey, I would be happy to keep an eye on your kids this afternoon, if that would be a help"—and Keith Richards or whoever it was would say, "Great! How would you like to come hear us practice?"

The Rolling Stone I would have been most likely to meet was Ron Wood. The house he rented was a quarter-mile up the road and around a corner from ours. At the time, it was a slightly scary-looking stucco mansion that had been on the market for a long time. (It has since been sold, stripped of its stucco, and cov-ered with cedar shingles.) One day about a year before the Stones came, I pretended to be a potential buyer, because I wanted to see what it was like inside. (It was big, and a couple of the bedrooms had sixties-style shag carpeting.) Wood was a controversial tenant, because when one of the big oak doors inside the house proved to be somewhat balky in the humid weather, he had a carpenter saw several inches off the bottom. I never saw Wood himself, but I did see his car, a gold-plated Ferrari Testarossa. Well, actually, Wood's car was a Ford Taurus station wagon.

The house Mick Jagger rented was farther away. I once went to a Christmas party there and (appropriately, I guess, in retrospect) had a little too much to drink. I've never been inside the house Keith Richards rented, although it belongs to some people I sort of know and I've driven past it many times. Charlie Watts and Bill Wyman stayed at a Ramada Inn about half an hour away. At first I worried that those two old-looking guys were staying in a motel because they had squandered their rock-and-roll riches and could no longer afford to rent big houses. But it turned out that after twenty-five years on the road they had simply become addicted to room service and cable TV.

The defunct girls' boarding school, where the Stones did their practicing, had become defunct the year before. My wife's stepgrandmother went there after the end of the First World War. She was the best student in the school one year, and her name was inscribed on a plaque that was still hanging in the room where the Stones did their practicing. The room had once been used for ballet recitals. While watching MTV later, I recognized it as the setting of one of the videos that the Stones released when their new album came out.

To keep down the noise while they were practicing and making their video, the Stones rented sixty-four rolls of fiberglass insulation from the local hardware store and hired a friend of mine to stack the rolls along the wall facing the road. I stopped along that road a few times late at night and either could or couldn't hear the Stones playing—I wasn't sure. But some friends of mine told me they heard them all the time.

When the Stones left, the rolls of insulation went back to the hardware store. Would you pay extra to wrap your house in pink fiberglass that had spent six weeks absorbing the music of the Rolling Stones? I would. I would pay 25 percent extra. Curiously, though, those rolls of insulation were sold for just their normal price.

# Home Again,
# Home Again

I GREW UP IN KANSAS CITY. When I return to visit my parents, I always make a point of driving past the little Dutch colonial on Huntington Road where we lived until I was seven. During our occupancy, the siding was white and the roof was green. In the thirty-five years since then, the house has undergone many transformations. The last time I saw it, the siding was pink and the roof was brown, and the little garage— on the roof of which my father once caught two neighborhood juvenile delinquents trying to burn my sister's and my Hula-Hoops with matches and a Coca-Cola bottle filled with gasoline— had been replaced by something grander. I've often been tempted to knock on the front door and ask to look around, but I've never actually done it. Would I really want to see what succeeding generations of home improvers have done to the backdrop of my earliest memories? I'm not certain that I would.

A few years ago, my parents moved out of the house where I spent the rest of my childhood and of which I have far more elaborate memories. I hadn't lived in the house for many years when they sold it, but I still felt proprietary. So did my children, who had visited their grandparents there several times and were deeply saddened by the thought of not being able to visit them there again. (Both my children hate changes of any kind. When my son was five, I tried to throw away a pair of socks that he had outgrown, and he cried, protesting, "I can still wear them on my hands!") Shortly after the new people moved in, a small fire started in the back of the house. The damage was confined to my old bedroom, which was destroyed. That news comforted me, for some reason. The total disappearance of my old room was easier to take than the idea of its being occupied by someone else.

My wife and I lived in Manhattan in the early eighties, when we were first married, and even now I go out of my way to walk past our old apartment building whenever I visit New York. The building has new windows, and I recognize only one of the doormen. We still exchange Christmas cards with a woman who lives in the apartment next to our old one. I could easily call her sometime and arrange to take a look inside our old place, but I never have. I guess I'm afraid that my memories of those years would begin to dissolve if I diluted them with actual knowledge of what has happened since.

Every so often, when I am working in my yard, I notice a familiar car driving slowly up our road. The car belongs to the man we bought the house from, in 1985. He now lives a couple of miles away. I never wave, because I'm pretty sure he doesn't know I recognize him. And I know better than to invite him inside for a closer look.

# Boneyard

**M**Y TOWN'S CEMETERY LIES just beyond the village green, about a half-mile from my house. It makes a convenient turnaround point on walks, and of course it has its own fascinations. The surnames on some of the older headstones are preserved also in the names of some of our older streets. There are graves of men and women who were born before the Revolution, and, especially in the older sections, there are numerous graves of children, many of whom died without names or had ages measured in months or days. Also buried in the cemetery are all three members of the family that lived in my house between 1850 and 1900: Erastus and Emmeline Hurlburt and their son, Egbert Erastus, who died before his second birthday. I often look for those graves first and try to draw from their headstones a poignant sense of my own end. But on nice summer days that's hard to do.

The subject of death doesn't always arise during walks in the cemetery, but it often does. When my son was two, he asked whether dead people come back to life. My wife said no.

"But children come back when they die," he said.

"No, they don't," my wife said. "But God takes them to live with Him in heaven."

"That's nice of God."

A few years earlier, my daughter had had a different reaction to the same concept. Her pet hamster had just died, and she said scornfully, "I wish she weren't *His* pet."

On a warm August morning when my son was three, the two of us walked to the green to buy coffee and a newspaper at the little general store, which has bankrupted a succession of genial proprietors. We stopped by the cemetery before returning home, and while I read the paper and drank my coffee, my son played on a small backhoe, which the father of a friend of mine would soon use to dig a grave for a woman I had met just once, at the hardware store. My son sat on the high seat and pretended to dig holes. There was a warning sticker next to the seat which said not to "hammer or beat sideways" with the bucket. My son asked me to read the warning to him several times, and he said that he would like to wait for my friend's father to return so that he could remind him not to do those things. After about an hour, I said that we could wait no longer. My son cried all the way home. He didn't cheer up until I suggested that he dig graves in our yard, and he later asked if I would buy him some "toy dirt" so that he could continue his excavations indoors.

Our yard was already a cemetery before my son began to dig there, and more graves have been added since. That old hamster of my daughter's is buried near the tree house, along with various mice, a hedgehog, a turtle, some fish, a parakeet, another hamster, and perhaps a dozen birds and chipmunks that never belonged to us but were judged worthy of full-blown funerals because they were victims of our cats. For a while, two white-rat cadavers lay side by side in plastic bags in the freezer compartment of the refrigerator in our basement. The rats died during the winter, when the ground was too hard for grave-digging, and had to be kept on ice until spring.

A few years ago, we thought we were going to have to dig a grave for one of our cats. He had slowed down and lost weight, and the vet said his kidneys were failing. We didn't know how old he was, because he had already been an adult when he wandered into our yard, about five years before. Then, one early-autumn morning, he didn't show up for breakfast.

My son later came across part of a small skeleton near the creek in the woods across the road. The bones were too small to be a cat's—they were probably a squirrel's—but we kept them anyway, and we still have them. We keep them next to the back door, on a flat stone near the steps, and we pay our respects as we come and go.

# AUTUMN

# A Second Home

ANY PEOPLE DREAM OF OWNING a second home. They picture a gray-shingled saltbox with a view of the ocean, or a cozy chalet near a ski slope in the mountains, or an old white farmhouse surrounded by orchards and stone walls.

I dream of owning a second home, too, but a different kind. Mine wouldn't be near the beach, or in the mountains, or at the end of a country road. It wouldn't be in a different state, or even a different town. It would be right up the street from my first home, maybe a couple of doors away.

My family's second home wouldn't look like the homes you see in a decorating magazine. It would be the kind of place where, when you go inside, you don't have to wipe your feet. The couch in the living room would not be white, and its cushions would not be stuffed with goose down. The chairs would be big, comfortable, and falling apart, like the ones in a fraternity house. The tables would be covered with Formica. We wouldn't have coasters, doormats, or fancy towels for guests. In our second home there would be no surface on which you could not put your feet.

The paint inside our second home would be so dark that handprints wouldn't show. Upstairs, each wall would have a hundred hooks, so that putting away clothes (and finding them later) would be easy. The sheets and pillowcases wouldn't match. Dart-boards and basketball hoops would hang from the backs of the bedroom doors. If our kids wanted to put up posters with mask-ing tape or thumbtacks or drywall screws, they wouldn't have to ask.

My wife and I, unlike most people, wouldn't use our second home for vacations. On a rainy autumn afternoon when our kids were bored, we'd say, "Why don't you guys run up to our second home and ride your bikes in the dining room?" We'd have all the birthday parties there, too, and all the sleepovers and poker games. We'd bathe the dog and clean fish in the kitchen sink. Rollerblading in the living room would be okay. If our kids wanted to hatch some chicks or make glass or build a papier-mâché volcano for the science fair at school, we'd send them up the street.

Our second home would be the place where we would go when we were tired of keeping up appearances. I wouldn't grit my teeth if I heard a door slam there. I wouldn't jump up if a gallon of milk hit the kitchen floor. Eating watermelon in the living room would be fine—just spit the seeds in the fireplace. I wouldn't yell at my kids for wiping their hands on the seats of the dining room chairs. I wouldn't fret about dents in the walls or dings in the floors or snowdrifts on the roof. The lawn would be weeds, and the kids could dig tunnels wherever they liked. If I needed to unload a bunch of groceries, I'd drive right across the yard to the back door.

In our second home, we would live the way people would live if they didn't care what other people might think. We would roughhouse and holler and throw things around. We wouldn't own antiques. And because our second home would be the home of all the messy parts of our lives, our first home would stay pretty nice. If we decided to have company for dinner one night, we wouldn't have to spend a frantic afternoon picking glitter and birdseed out of the dining room rug. All the glitter and birdseed would be up the street, at our other place. And that's where we would send our kids as soon as the guests began to arrive.

# Wildlife

O N A CRISP OCTOBER MORNING, my wife, while walking in some woods near our house, saw a flash of white among the stones in an old wall. A moment later, a small creature with pink eyes peered out and sniffed the air. It was a rat. My wife is an amateur rodentologist, and she figured that the odds against finding an albino *Rattus norvegicus* in the wild must be incalculably huge. As she marveled in silence, another white rat emerged. Then another and another. With a pang of disappointment she realized that what she had stumbled across was not an exotic genetic enclave but, in all likelihood, the abandoned subjects of some local teenager's science-fair project.

Come to think of it, there is quite a bit of semidomestic wildlife around here. The walls of my house are filled not only with dust, broken chunks of plaster, and no insulation, but also with several million mice. The mice are inconspicuous during the day, but at night they sound like badgers on roller skates. Shortly after we moved in, I went to the hardware store and bought a case of rodent poison. "Feeding your animals?" the clerk asked. I conscientiously fed them for several months. Then, on the day of the year's first snow, I pulled my winter boots out of the coat closet and discovered that one of them was half full of rodent poison. The mice had been collecting it for months and storing it for future consumption. A short time later, my wife and I bought some of those traps that catch mice without killing them. We caught two or three mice every day for a week and let them go in the yards of people we didn't like.

At around the same time, a local newspaper ran a story about a man who said he had seen a small bear rummaging on his porch. The newspaper reported the man's story without comment, but his description made it clear that the beagle-sized creature he had seen eating his dog's dinner was not a bear but a raccoon. There is a raccoon that visits our cat's bowl almost every evening, and when it runs away after being startled it looks very much like a long-tailed miniature bear. In contrast, the skunk and possum who share the cat's dinner with the raccoon look very much like a skunk and possum.

You might think that the cat would help with our mouse problem, but the mice live inside and the cat lives outside. In fact, the mice may be scared to leave. If so, they are the only animals in our care who exhibit anxiety in any form. The deer who eat our bushes and graze on our lawn don't look up anymore when we slam the back door. A friend visiting from New York City recently assumed that the fawn he saw standing in the children's sandbox was a pet. The day after our first Christmas in our house, my mother, who was visiting with my father, spotted three deer in the yard at six-thirty in the morning and went running through the house like a madwoman. She wasn't used to seeing deer. The deer, however, were used to human voices. They continued with their breakfast while my daughter, who was eighteen months old, watched them from the front steps and asked me many questions.

"No?"

"Yes," I said, "the deer have noses."

"Eye?"

"Yes, the deer have eyes."

"Eee?"

"Yes, the deer have ears."

"Tee?"

"Yes, the deer have tails."

"Doggy?"

"Yes, dogs have tails, too."

"Mommy?"

"No, Mommy doesn't have a tail."

"Poo-poo?"

"The deer go poo-poo outside."

"Daddy?"

"Daddy goes poo-poo in the toilet."

"Mimi?"

"Mimi goes poo-poo in the toilet, too."

Where various people and animals poop was one of my daughter's key interests at that time. Back in New York, we had used to say, "Mimi goes poo-poo in a box," because in those days Mimi was our neighbor's cat and not my brother's wife. My wife made me stop saying, "Grammie goes poo-poo in Kansas City" instead of "Grammie goes poo-poo in the toilet" because she thought that confused our daughter, who in those days thought that my parents lived in the little stone house at the end of our road. (She knew that the house was a house, and she had been told that my parents lived in a house, so she drew the obvious conclusion.)

The possums pay even less attention to us than the deer. A couple of years ago, one of them fell into one of our garbage cans and couldn't climb out. I tipped the can on its side and went back into the house. When I took some trash out a couple of hours later, the possum was still there. It was sitting in the bottom of the garbage can, staring at me, and no doubt wondering why I had taken so long to bring it something to eat.

# Anatomy of a Kitchen

L IKE MOST HOMEOWNERS, I sometimes come across remodeling ideas in magazines. Usually, though, I find that the magazines and I are on different wavelengths, and that the beautiful, idealized rooms depicted in their pages don't speak to my needs. For example, there never seem to be any gym shoes on the microwave ovens in any of the kitchens. That leads me to wonder where the owners of the kitchens store their children's possessions. Inside their refrigerators, perhaps?

The features of my own kitchen are less picturesque but possibly of greater interest to the average reader. Here are some of them:

- *The plate compactor.* This appliance, when empty, looks like an ordinary sink, but it is far more useful. A few years ago I discovered that once a pile of dirty dishes has reached a certain height, the dishes near the bottom will gradually become almost clean all by themselves. I can't explain the phenomenon. It may be related to the high-pressure process that turns anthracite into diamonds. An additional benefit: keeping all the dishes, glasses, and silverware in one place simplifies table setting. A quick rinse under the tap makes everything ready to go again.

- *The counter quilt.* It isn't always possible to fit all the dishes into the plate compactor, especially after a big dinner party or holiday feast. On such occasions, I stack the overflow on the countertop or the range. Such piles are unsightly, however. Having to elbow your way past greasy pans the next morning just to get at the coffeemaker can be depressing. I postpone this unsettling moment by temporarily hiding the mess beneath an old blanket that our dog sometimes sleeps on. The blanket gives the counter a cheerful, homey look, like that of a freshly made bed.

- *Plate levelers.* I often eat my lunch at the kitchen table. Because the table is usually covered with newspapers, magazines, schoolwork, old art projects, crayons, colored markers, overdue library books, and yesterday's junk mail, I sometimes have trouble making my plate and glass sit perfectly flat. To correct the problem, I use my son's comic books as shims. Three or four are usually enough to level and stabilize a complete place setting.

- *The fifty-five-gallon garbage can.* Most kitchen wastebaskets are too small to be truly useful. They are also so short that even a dachshund can easily nose open the top and make a quick snack of coffee grounds, chicken bones, and paper towels. For that reason, I last year got rid of our old foot-pedal wastebasket and purchased a replacement from an industrial-supply company. The new receptacle is four feet tall, is bright red, and has the international BIOHAZARD symbol on its side. Its lid is the size of a manhole cover and can be used as an alternate work surface when the counters and table are in use.

Our kitchen isn't finished yet. I still haven't figured out how best to accommodate our two prairie dogs, who live in a stove-sized cage next to an old bureau in which we store birdseed, cat food, and aluminum foil. The problem is that the prairie dogs enjoy shredding cloth napkins, which I can never seem to remember not to place on top of their cage. Undoubtedly there is a simple solution. Perhaps I will discover it in a future issue of a home-improvement magazine.

# Renovation Inertia

O NE'S ENTHUSIASM FOR HOME-RENOVATION projects generally conforms to Newton's first law of motion: A project at rest tends to remain at rest, while a project in motion tends to remain in motion unless acted upon by an outside agency (such as a hysterical loan officer). Overcoming home-improvement inertia can be difficult. For example, I almost never get around to cleaning my gutters, because clogged gutters aren't a problem during nice weather, when it would be easy for me to clean them, and I hate to climb a ladder in the rain.

Similarly, major remodeling projects can take forever to begin. A new kitchen would be nice, but do you really want to eat at McDonald's for three months while the work is being done? Merely thinking about having to vacuum joint-compound dust out of your electrical outlets can make you reluctant to put the job out for bids.

Once home-improvement projects are under way, though, they have a tendency to go on forever—and not only because of incompetence, mistakes, and delays. Having contractors around the house can be extremely seductive. As long as there are big strong guys with power tools on the premises, why not ask them to tear apart the laundry room as well? And why not ask them to fix that broken garage door? And how about a small shed for firewood? It usually takes me a long time to call a plumber or an electrician, but once I have him in my house he begins to seem like family and I never want to let him go.

I often face this situation with painters. I tend to postpone painting projects, because I hate spending money on something that's just going to have to be done again. But as soon as the painters are here, I think of dozens of extra projects for them to do. Let's paint the basement! Let's paint the basement stairs! Let's paint the basement floor!

Hired workers, even more than children and pets, give a house an atmosphere of cheerful industry, of sensible plans being carried to completion. I once hired a carpenter to do some trim work on the third floor of my house. For two or three days, we worked within chatting distance of each other, I at my desk and he just outside my office door. We talked about this and that, and I spent a lot of time looking over his shoulder as he performed various complicated procedures involving chisels, planes, and saws. I didn't get much done. Then again, neither did he. Still, we both had a wonderful time. If he had been paying me, instead of the other way around, my happiness would have been complete.

Even more satisfying than the companionship of hired workers is the fact that their efforts produce tangible results. At the end of the day, your house doesn't look the same as it did when you woke up: the element of surprise. I like to steer clear of the work site for as long as I can bear to, and take a peek. Perhaps some walls will have been painted a different color, or a floor will have been torn up and taken to the dump. What I do for a living doesn't make much of a dent in my physical environment; what they do does. On several occasions, my wife and I have left our house in the hands of various workers while we went on vacation. Driving home two weeks later, I tingled with anticipation. Will the job be finished? Will the old roof be gone? Will the house have burned to the ground?

Having lots of workers on the premises is like having one of those big, old-fashioned extended families that made life in the olden days so much more wholesome than life today. I like learning about my workers' children and marital problems, and I like making educated guesses about their personal habits based on the stuff I see strewn in the backs of their trucks. I am interested in what they bring to eat for lunch. I never want them to go away.

# Anybody There?

WHEN I WAS LITTLE, my parents had a single telephone. It sat in a small, peculiar niche in the front hall, and it didn't ring very often. We moved when I was in second grade. Our new house had two phones, one in the kitchen and one in my parents' bedroom. Those two phones lasted us until I was in high school, when an extension was added to my room. I would call my girlfriend at night, and we would chat in a desultory way whenever nothing interesting was happening on whatever television show she was watching at the same time. I suppose my sister must have received an extension, too, a couple of years later, when she herself became a brooding adolescent. I knew a few kids whose families had a second line, but not many. It never seemed like that big a deal.

I just did a census of the phones in my house and found thirteen, plus one stand-alone fax machine, four fax/modems and three answering machines. We have four lines—two for voice, one for fax, one for the Internet. (Surprisingly, perhaps, we don't have a cell phone or even a regular portable.) Lately, I've begun to think that we would be prudent to add another line or two. I have a four-line phone in my office, and there are times when all four lights are lit.

A strong proponent of increasing the family's bandwidth is my daughter, who discovered the phone in a big way when she was in seventh grade. That year, she and her friends spent essentially all their time debating by telephone whether one or another of them ought or ought not to be "going out" with one or another of the boys. I use quotation marks because the activity in question involved neither "going" nor "out."

Here's what happened. One of the girls would set her sights on one of the boys and ask him if he would like to "go out." He would say that he would not. Dire notes would be passed among the girls, and secret meetings would be held. A committee of the girl's advisers would track down the boy after class and confront him with evidence that he and the girl were perfect for each other. The boy, seeing no escape, would relent. The girls would celebrate. The next day, the boy would decide that, although he would never have chosen this fate for himself, he would be a poor sport not to act the part, and he would wait in the hallway to walk with the girl to lunch. She would find his attention alarming and disgusting, and angrily brush past him. The next day, the girl— after sobbing with her advisers on the telephone far into the night—would break up with him, often through an intermediary. Not infrequently, she would also inform him that she hated him.

A year or so later, the boys got hormones, too, and the stakes were irrevocably raised. When my daughter was in seventh grade, though, I was good at giving advice. She would put down the phone and say to me in anguish that Heidi and Kyle, for example, didn't seem to be getting along, and I knew exactly what to say: "I think they ought to break up."

# Work Marriage

I DON'T WORK IN A REGULAR OFFICE, so I miss out on a lot of things that people who do don't, such as a new pen whenever I want one, coffee breaks, comical stories about my dumb boss, the concept of the weekend, lunchtime Jazzercize with my coworkers, a mysteriously burgeoning colony of Sweet'n Low packets in my desk, nice clothes for daytime wear, and work marriage.

Work marriage is a relationship that exists between certain people of the opposite sex who work at the same place. For example, let's say that you, like me, are a man. In that case your work wife would be the woman in your office who:

(a) as you walk past her desk on your way to a big meeting, tells you that you have dried shaving cream behind your ear

(b) has lunch with you pretty often

(c) returns stuff that she borrows from your desk

(d) tells you things about her other (home) husband that he wouldn't want you to know

(e) waits for you to finish up so that you can go down in the elevator together

(f) complains to you without embarrassment about an uncomfortable undergarment

(g) expects you to tell the truth, more or less, about the thing she has done to her hair

(h) thinks you eat, drink, and smoke an acceptable amount

(i) knows at least one thing about you—such as the fact that you can do a pretty good imitation of Liza Minnelli—that your home wife doesn't know.

Work marriage is, in some ways, better than home marriage. For example, your work wife would never ask you why you don't just put your dishes right into the dishwasher instead of leaving them in the sink—she doesn't know you do it! Also, she would never wedge your car between two others in the parking lot at Bradlees, sign you up to be the pie auctioneer at a church bazaar, or grab hold of your stomach and ask, "What's this? Blubber?" She knows you only as you appear between nine and five: recently bathed, fully dressed, largely awake, and in control of your life.

My wife and I both work at home. In that sense, I guess, my home wife is also my work wife. And yet this cannot be. Our argument about whether rapidly changing channels hurts the TV does not disappear at nine o'clock on Monday morning. Like many other self-employed (and thus work-single) people, I am forced to content myself with fleeting and ultimately unsatisfying pseudo work marriages, such as my relationship with a checkout girl at the grocery store. She has a pretty good idea of what I like to eat, and I help her out sometimes by doing my own bagging, but that's about as far as it goes. (Perhaps I have merely discovered a new, less-committed type of relationship: store dating. There is also the brief but intense infatuation one feels for an attractive person whose car one has just passed on a highway.)

The only way to have a real work marriage is, sadly, to work. Sure, I'd like a work wife someday—*someday*. But I'm not willing, right now, to get a regular job in order to have one. There are just too many things about offices (no dogs or children, no nap whenever you want one, parking problems) that rub me the wrong way. For the time being, I guess, my home wife will have to do.

# When *Was* the Past?

T HE SMALL NEW ENGLAND TOWN where I live was incorporated in 1779. It has a picture-book village green, which is shaded by enormous maple trees and bordered by very old houses. In the middle of the green is a Congregational church that was rebuilt, after a fire, in 1800. The houses and the church are painted white, and they have black shutters. Every autumn, the big maples carpet the ground with red and orange leaves, and busloads of tourists come to gape.

A few years ago, a boarding school whose campus abuts one corner of the green petitioned my town's historical commission for permission to remove three old signs and erect seven new ones. The new signs, which would identify various driveways leading into the campus, would be small and tastefully designed. Unlike the old signs, they would all be the same size and color. None of the new signs would be placed on the green itself, but two or three would be fairly near it.

The school's petition created an uproar. You might as well fill the green with billboards, some people grumbled. In the weeks that followed, the issue was debated and tabled and debated again, and it wasn't decided for months. (The new signs finally went up.) At a public meeting, a man I know made an impassioned speech in which he described the green as "a perfectly preserved early-nineteenth-century gem." Many people in my town agree. They argued that any but the most minor alteration would be a desecration.

The flaw in this argument was that it wasn't true. My town's two-hundred-year-old green, while certainly a gem, belongs mostly to the twentieth century. A hundred and fifty years ago, the oldest white house on the green was painted red. The house just east of it was painted yellow, and the house just west of it was a store with a big porch in front where customers could loiter. There was a cigar factory (with a big sign), and there were barns and a blacksmith shop. Chickens wandered among the houses. There was a baseball diamond—a photograph of which is reproduced in the endpapers of the coffee-table book *Baseball: An Illustrated History*, by Geoffrey C. Ward and Ken Burns—where the maples are now. (The trees were added in the 1950s, with the help of a big crane.) The Congregational parish house was a fraction of its current size. The main road ran in a different place. A landmark house, which now has a mansard roof and a beautiful Palladian window, was then just a basic colonial box. The house next door (which was built by a rich antipapist, who was determined to fill every building lot on the green so that the town's Catholics would have nowhere to build a church) wasn't there.

In other words, my town's perfect early-nineteenth-century green really looks very little like its true early-nineteenth-century self. It is a modern idea of what an old green ought to look like. There's nothing wrong with that. In fact, I prefer the modern version to the squalid, rough-hewn original, at least as a backdrop for my modern life. But we should remember that when we look at the past we can see it only from the vantage point of the present. Questions about historical accuracy aren't always black and white. Sometimes they are yellow and red.

# Virtual Friends

TELECOMMUTING WOULD CATCH ON faster if you could do it from a regular office. That way you could combine the best parts of working at home (daytime movies, faxing in your underpants, postbreakfast napping) with the best parts of working in a faceless monolith of glass, concrete, and steel (free pens, free phone calls, secretarial intrigue). As a long-time telecommuter, I've wrestled with this problem for years. A few years ago, I found a partial solution: I became a compulsive viewer of CNBC, the cable-television network that covers business all day long.

CNBC has a lot to offer the homebound worker, including thoughtful speculation about the direction of interest rates and stock prices that glide continually along the bottom of the screen, even during commercials. What I love about it, though, is not its content but its companionship. I have come to view the members of the CNBC staff as my home-office coworkers.

Turning on my TV the first thing in the morning is like coming in to work early and putting my feet up on my desk. Running CNBC in the background makes my home office seem not like a solitary prison cell or torture chamber but like a beehive of cheerful, important activity. No matter how unmotivated I may feel about doing my own job, the people on the screen seem enthusiastic and engaged, even if all they're doing is discussing a sudden small decrease in the number of yen to the deutsche mark. If I lose interest in some project of my own, I lean back and watch CNBC until I feel like making money again. If I really have to buckle down, I press the mute button on my remote control— the electronic equivalent of closing my office door—but I never turn off the TV.

Virtual coworkers are better than flesh-and-blood coworkers in several respects: They are paid to be entertaining, they are always in the same mood, and they never duck into the bathroom when they see you coming down the hall. Most of the people at CNBC seem to me to be about my age (which means, I suppose, that they are five or ten years younger), and some of the guys don't wear jackets. There's quite a bit of kidding around, even with the CEOs of big companies. I can nurse my powerful crushes on Sue Herera and Maria Bartiromo without endangering my marriage or risking accusations of sexual harassment. (I'm pretty sure Sue Herera has a thing for me, too, although it's difficult to read the body language of someone whose body usually ends at her armpits.) The only guys in the office I never liked were Dan Dorfman and a guy who smiled too much and always nodded when he talked; both have been let go.

Now that I have begun to settle in to my job with the folks at CNBC, I realize that I have had other virtual office mates during my career. For example, I now think of CNN's coverage of the Persian Gulf War—which I watched obsessively—not as a special news program but as an exciting start-up company that I used to work for. In those heady days, I loved going to my office, and I often stayed there late into the night. There was also a period during 1995 and 1996 when I took a leave from CNBC to fill in as an assistant prosecutor on a big murder case out in L.A.

CNBC is not the perfect virtual office. There's no health plan, most of the men wear makeup, and I don't know who our boss is. I wouldn't presume to tinker very much, though. I might add an after-hours segment set in a bar. It would be like Cheers, but the people having drinks would be Joe Kernen, David Faber, Ron Insana, and all my other best buddies from the regular show. I might also add a whole separate channel about the receptionists and mail-room guys, who invariably know the best dirt. In a decade or two, perhaps, CNBC will be available in a holographic format that will make the show appear to take place not on my television screen but in my actual office, at desks right next to mine.

I realize I'm probably making it sound as though all I do is work. Believe me, I don't. Today was a good example. At three o'clock this afternoon, a full hour before the closing bell on Wall Street, I said good-bye to the guys at the office and went over to ESPN for a round of golf.

# Benign Neglect

SHORTLY BEFORE MY WIFE AND I closed the deal for our house, I had a mild attack of the suddenly incapacitating illness known as buyer's remorse. The issue was the garage. The rear wall, which was made of concrete blocks and set into the side of a hill, was bowing inward, and there were several large cracks through which one could see tree roots or daylight or both. Intoxicated by the thought of all the money I was about to spend, I hadn't noticed this myself. The wall's convexity had to be pointed out to me by a professional home inspector, who found it alarming.

The seller was coldly unsympathetic when I suggested that we use the imploding garage as an excuse to reduce his asking price to a sum I could afford. The garage was fifteen years old, he said. It had always bulged like that, and the problem—if any— was merely cosmetic, so let's get on with the deal. I got the impression from his defensive tone that he had probably built the garage himself, and that he stood by his original decision to erect the rear wall without reinforcement or drainage. At the real estate agent's suggestion, I asked a local builder to take a look. The builder said that the wall might last for twenty years or it might fall down tomorrow but that any money spent trying to shore it up would be a waste.

As things turned out, my buyer's remorse went into remission and we bought the house, bulge and all, for the price already agreed upon. I checked my automobile-insurance policy to be sure it covered body damage caused by falling chunks of concrete, then sat back to await the inevitable collapse.

Well, it's more than a dozen years later and I'm still waiting. The bulge is noticeably worse than it was when we moved in, and some of the cracks are now large enough to hide heirlooms in, but the wall is inexplicably still standing. My faith in gravity has been shaken.

But I've learned something interesting: An utterly neglected structure takes a heck of a lot longer to fall apart than you might expect. From a hundred feet away, my garage still looks pretty good, even though I've never lifted a finger to maintain it. Not wanting to throw good money after bad, I have never painted it, washed it, pruned the trees that overhang it, patched the roof, chased out the community of squirrels that lives among the rafters, or cleaned the gutters, which are clogged with tree litter, pine needles, weeds, and several hundred small but robust maple saplings. I did once repair some volleyball-sized holes in the doors, but that's it. My total investment in maintenance amounts to about two dollars per year.

What if you painted your house every twenty years instead of every seven? What if you never cleaned your gutters? What if you unplugged your sump pump and let the water in your basement find its own level? What if you let your lawn grow wild until the neighbors complained? What if you adopted a live-and-let-live policy toward your termites?

You wouldn't want to push these ideas too far. After thirty years or so, your house would probably be a big, leaky mess. In the short term, though, your life would be vastly easier, not to mention less expensive. No more trips to the hardware store!

No more weekend chores! And best of all, if you timed everything right, you would leave all the really big problems for the next guy.

# The Perfect Job

T HE PERFECT JOB—the one you could have if you could have any job in the world—what would it be?

The most nearly perfect part of any less-than-perfect job is usually the occasional hour in which you are able to pretend that you are doing the job but in fact you are reading a magazine and eating candy. The rest of the office is throbbing frantically, but you are sitting quietly at your desk and learning interesting facts about a guy who put his wife in a wood chipper. The perfect job would feel like that, but all the time.

The trouble with less-than-perfect jobs is that they usually don't swoop you up and fling you through your day. That is, you don't very often look up at the clock to find out how many minutes past eleven it is and discover that it's five and time to go home. That's what the perfect job would be like. The time would zoom by, the way it does when you are going through some old boxes and suddenly discover that they are filled with artifacts from the Pilgrim days.

Well, I've thought about this a lot (while I was supposed to be doing something else), and I've narrowed down my choice of perfect job to five possibilities:

- Doing an unbelievably great cleanup of my basement, and organizing my workshop so that I know exactly where everything is, and drawing up a lot of plans to show how I might expand my workshop so that it would fill the entire basement instead of just a third of it, and buying every conceivable kind of woodworking tool and finding exactly the perfect place to keep each one, but never actually getting around to doing any woodworking projects.

• Doing the *Times* crossword puzzle and watching MTV while listening to people I knew in college discuss their marital problems on the other side of a one-way mirror.

• Sorting my son's vast Lego collection—by type, size, and color—into muffin tins and other containers while my son nearby happily builds vehicles and structures without getting bored or saying he wants something to eat.

• Setting the prison sentences of criminals convicted in highly publicized court cases; making all parole decisions for these people; receiving daily updates on how they spend their time in jail.

• Touring the houses of strangers and looking through their things while they're not there. If I were driving along and happened to see a house that looked interesting, I could pull over and let myself in with a set of master keys. If the people happened to be there, I would spray them with a harmless paralyzing gas that would prevent them from remembering that I had read their diaries and checked to see whether they were making efficient use of their limited amount of storage space, which they probably wouldn't have been.

All these jobs, as I see them, would require a full complement of office supplies: every conceivable kind of clip and clasp, name-brand ballpoint pens, ungunked-up bottles of correction fluid, ammolike refills for various desktop mechanisms, and cool, smooth, hard pads of narrow-lined paper. I guess I would also need a high-speed computer network, a fancy copier, and a staff of cheerful recent college graduates eager to do my bidding. Plus a really great benefits program that would pay not only for doctors and prescription drugs but also for things like deodorant.

Recently, I've begun to think that my *real* perfect job would probably consist of all five of my *possible* perfect jobs, one for each weekday. That way I would never have to lie awake at night wondering whether sorting my son's Legos would have made me happier than snooping through people's tax returns. Then, on weekends, I could hang around my house, drinking beer and watching college football on TV. I would seem to be having a really great time, but in reality I would be counting the hours until Monday and just itching to get back to work.

# Clicking

WHEN MY SON WAS EIGHT, we set out one day to determine the main reason why we were glad we live now and not two hundred years ago. I considered antibiotics, air travel, the telephone, central heating, Proust, the automobile, alternating current, and anesthesia before settling, finally, on toilet paper.

My son was less conflicted. Without a moment's hesitation he said, "My computer."

It's easy to lose track of how rapidly the world changes. I can make both my children shudder simply by describing my first computer. It was one of the first IBM PCs, purchased in 1981. It came with 64K of RAM, an allotment that today looks like a typographical error. "Floppy disks were really floppy in those days," I tell my kids, prompting howls of disbelief, "and there were no hard drives, and nothing was in color." Way back then, suddenly having the ability to repair a spelling mistake without using correction fluid made me feel more modern than George Jetson. Sixteen years later—with E-mail, desktop publishing, on-line banking, and the Internet—I have trouble recreating the sense of astonishment I felt as I first watched a sentence I was typing jump to the next line without the intervention of a carriage return key.

Today my house contains six computers—one for each member of the family, plus two laptops. To anyone whose home is still computer-free, that must seem like ludicrous excess. But our computers get far more use than any of our other appliances, including the TVs, and there are times when even half a dozen seems like less than enough. Each of my children now views a computer as a nonnegotiable entitlement, like a trip to Disney World.

The future always eludes prediction, but when I watch my children at their machines I occasionally feel as though I'm catching a glimpse of what's ahead. My kids, unlike most of the grown-ups I know, don't brood about the "complexity" of their computers. If anything, they yearn for further complications: they want bigger hard drives, more powerful printers, faster modems, better graphics cards, more breathtaking central processors. They install new programs fearlessly, even recklessly, and then they poke and prod and nudge and shove until they have figured out how to use them. When my daughter was twelve, she mentioned that she would like her own page on the World Wide Web. I said I didn't know what was involved but that I would consult various references and see what I could find out—the standard middle-aged response. A couple of hours later, she told me not to bother. On her own she had just created and launched a five-page Web site—including a threaded message board, a picture of the cast of the television show *ER*, and a link to the site of an animal-rights organization—using a program I had figured was over my head.

Adults often complain that computers are harder to use than television sets. My children, and yours, would likely respond, "So what?" When I asked my daughter how she had learned to make her Web page, she shrugged. "I just clicked everything," she said. In terms of what the world will look like fifteen years from now, it doesn't matter that you and I can't figure out these contraptions. Their role in our culture, and in the homes of our children, will not be created by us.

# Rooms with Views

O NE AUTUMN DAY, while I was in the throes of a powerful urge to spend a lot of money belonging to a bank, I
went with a real estate agent to look at a piece of land.
The building site had heart-stopping views that extended virtually
to the Southern Hemisphere. I could see mist-shrouded hills and
sun-dappled valleys, and I was nearly overcome by yearning. I
imagined myself reclining in front of the thirty-room villa I would
build on that very spot, gazing contentedly into neighboring states.

Then I snapped out of it and went back to my regular life.
For a while I felt pretty rich, because a family of four could live
comfortably on the difference between what I earn and what I
would have had to earn to pay for that villa. Eventually, though, I
started feeling poor again. Then I began to rationalize. What's
the big deal about views anyway?

One little-discussed fact about impressive views is that they
are not permanent. Like most nice things, they wear out with
use. The first time you stand on your porch and run your eyes
over the curvature of the earth, the scene takes your breath away.
The thousandth time you do it, your lungs scarcely notice. Famil-
iarity inexorably turns the transcendent into a cliché—like the
*Mona Lisa*. The more you look, the less you see.

People who build houses on breathtaking lots often squan-
der their views in their efforts to possess them. They build huge

windows and glass doors and sprawling balconies and porches, and they orient the important rooms to maintain an unblinking vigil on whatever there is to see. The result, paradoxically, is that the view evaporates at an accelerated rate. Because it is always on display, it quickly loses its ability to surprise.

The most effective way to preserve a view is to be stingy with it. A small window will hold a good view longer than a two-story wall made of glass. It keeps its power in part because it demands some effort from the viewer, the way a book does. For the same reason, a long view lasts longer if you have to look around a tree or over a wall to see it. A view should flirt with the viewer rather than baldly proposition. It should leave something to the imagination.

The same instinct for grandiloquence that leads people to build glass walls also creates a powerful bias in favor of long views over short ones. But is a snowcapped mountain on a distant horizon necessarily more stirring than an old barn in the next field, or a stone wall at the end of the yard, or an apple tree twenty feet away, or, for that matter, a flowerpot standing on the windowsill? One of my favorite views at my house is also one of the shortest: just some old weeds and wildflowers on a little rise, viewed through an old window with wavy glass, best seen while lying on the couch. Nor does a good view have to have anything natural about it. When we lived in New York, I loved gazing at the apartment building across the street. We had some friends who bragged about their unobstructed view of the Brooklyn Bridge, but my view—a hundred big windows with real people behind them—was a lot more interesting to look at day in and day out.

The best way to handle views might be to display them on a rotating basis, like pictures in a museum. You could close the shutters on half your windows on New Year's Day, then switch to the other half on the Fourth of July. At the very least, we should all remember that what we look at is less important than what we see.

# How to Get Rich Quick

**M**OST PEOPLE ARE RICH in some ways (good health, happy outlook, stimulating hobbies) but not in others (money). Ordinarily I'm not a complainer, but hearing about people who are rich in the money way sometimes makes me grouchy. Not long ago, I decided to do something about it.

My wife and I know some people who have a house in the country (as we do) and an apartment in New York (as we don't). After talking to these people one day, I asked myself, Does the fact that we have only one place to live mean we're poor? A few days later, I found myself browsing through the real estate section of the Sunday *New York Times*. Buried in the fine print on page 78 was an advertisement that caught my eye. It was for an eight-room duplex apartment with two regular bedrooms, a maid's room, a laundry room, and a terrace on the forty-eighth and forty-ninth floors of a building in a fancy neighborhood in Manhattan. By regular house standards this apartment was a little on the dinky size, but by New York standards it was palatial. A once-in-a-lifetime opportunity! Most of all, I liked the rent: twelve thousand five hundred dollars a month. That works out to a hundred and fifty thousand dollars a year.

So here's what I did: I didn't rent it. Not doing that gave my wife and me an extra hundred and fifty grand a year to spend on anything we like. That's not enough to make us *rich* rich, but it's enough to make us darned comfortable. And not renting that apartment had an unanticipated benefit: unlike certain people we know, we don't have to spend half our time driving our screaming children back and forth between our place in the city and our place in the country.

A short time later, while my wife and I were still just nouveaux riches, I saw one of those Mercedes-Benz station wagons. It was parked in front of the liquor store. The car was so new that it still had the dealer's price sticker in the window. Do you know what the manufacturer's suggested retail price was? It was almost a hundred thousand dollars.

I was shocked. My wife and I had a station wagon at the time, but it was just one of the normal brands. It had a front seat, a backseat, and a "way back," just like the Mercedes, yet it cost only about a fifth as much. I did some quick, on-the-spot arithmetic and decided not to trade up—a deal that left more than seventy thousand dollars on the table for my wife and me.

Incidentally, my wife and I park our cars in our driveway. We have a garage, but it's too full of junk to use for anything but storing junk. Neither the driveway nor the garage cost us anything. They came free when we bought our house. If we had rented that apartment in New York, though, we wouldn't have had a free place to park during our hectic, noise-filled visits. We would have had to pay exorbitant Manhattan rates for a spot in a nearby garage. Then—merely in order to duplicate what we get now for nothing—we would have had to rent at least three more spaces for our trash cans, old tires, squirrels, and so on, plus another space for our other car, which we might want to bring to the city every once in a while on a whim. (When we first moved to the country, we tried to get by with only one car, but we rapidly realized that if you don't have a second car, you can't get to the repair shop to pick it up after one of you has driven it into a big rock.)

The really great thing is, the rich really do keep getting richer. Not long ago, my wife and I celebrated our wedding anniversary by forgetting it for several days and then, unlike certain people we know, not spending a couple of weeks alone on a fabulous exotic tropical island. A trip like that could easily cost twenty grand—money we simply added to our pile.

As we did, I couldn't help but feel a little smug about the level of affluence we had attained. I was also reminded of something that a wealthy friend once told me. The secret of happiness, he said, is to have poor friends.

# WINTER

# Being Prepared

W HEN THE FIRST SNOW FALLS in my part of the country, I look down into the woods across the road from
my house and I think about what I always think
about at this time of year: power failures. Almost every winter we
have three or four. The big winds blow, and somewhere along
one of the little highways that winds among the hills a snow-
laden tree branch snaps and a power line breaks, and the lights
go out in half a dozen little towns.

Typically, this happens in the middle of the night and when
the temperature is close to zero. When our kids were little, my
wife and I could tell right away that the power was gone, because
our son and daughter, who could sleep through anything else,
would begin to howl the instant their night-lights went out. Now
it's usually the temperature that wakes us. The walls in our house
are mostly just for show. Zero-degree weather doesn't take long
to finger its way inside.

Our first power failure—which happened a few months after
we moved in—seemed like an adventure. I had happy memories
of childhood blackouts: candlelight flickering in the kitchen,
sleeping bags spread in front of the fireplace, flashlight beams
darting in the neighbors' windows. But my first blackout as a
homeowner didn't seem like fun for long. Shortly after our lights
came back on, I realized that the water in a baseboard radiator in

our living room had frozen. The pipe took most of two days to thaw, and during that time the downstairs remained chilly. Then, suddenly, hot water was spewing like a geyser across the floor. It soaked a nice rug and cascaded into the basement through gaps between the old floorboards. I later realized that ice had burst the pipe, then acted as a plug. The torrent didn't begin until the furnace had come back on and gradually thawed the pipe.

With each succeeding winter, I learned a little more about how to cope. I bought two backup night-lights that plugged in to wall outlets and came on if the power went off. I packed insulation around the exposed radiator pipes that run just inside the top of my house's foundation, and I had a plumber add anti-freeze to the water in the heating pipes. I bought a gasoline-powered generator, and when it turned out to be too wimpy I bought another. I hired an electrician to install a device next to my service panel that automatically isolates my generator from the main power line, so that I won't endanger the lives of linemen working to restore my power by inadvertently feeding current back into the lines. The device also lets me pick and choose among five important household circuits: the ones that supply our furnace, well pump, refrigerator and freezer, microwave oven, and a handful of downstairs lights.

The first winter my system was fully operational, I rubbed my hands in anticipation. I changed the oil in the generator, laid in a new stock of flashlight batteries, and waited for the season to do its worst. Weeks went by. Then months. Big snows fell, but the power lines didn't snap. After brooding about power failures for close to six years, and after spending roughly fifteen hundred dollars on remedies, I now had a new worry: What if the lights never went out again?

# A Creature Was Stirring

M Y WIFE AND I OUGHT TO WRITE one of those best-selling books about how to train dogs. We bought a dachshund puppy, and we decided to bring it up right. Our previous dog had been loyal, playful, and affectionate, but it had never, in its fifteen years with us, exhibited much in the way of discipline. We bought the new puppy a crate to sleep in, as all best-selling dog books recommend, and we decided that our new pet, unlike its predecessor, would never be allowed to climb on the furniture.

The first night home, the puppy whimpered in its crate for a little while before falling asleep. The second night, it cried for an hour or two. The third night, it howled for quite a while. The fourth night, it howled continuously, beginning at about ten. "This can't go on," I said, shaking my fist in the darkness. Reluctantly, my wife agreed. Trembling with rage, I marched down-stairs, snatched the pup from its crate, brought it upstairs, and thrust it under the covers. It has slept with us every night since then, and it hasn't howled once. When people have trouble with pets, it's usually because they don't know how to be firm.

Even though the dog has now learned its lesson, there's still plenty of noise in our house after dark. If you stand at the head of the stairs at midnight, you can hear what sounds like a bicycle being ridden on its rims inside a cement mixer full of ball bearings. That's our two hamsters, our vole, and our four mice working out on their exercise wheels. Many people, hearing the metallic screeching, would be annoyed, but to me the galloping rodents make a homey, comforting music. Besides, I figure that any burglar sticking his head through one of our windows at night would be unsettled by the racket and would decide to check out our next-door neighbor instead.

No house is silent, whether or not it contains pets. At this time of year, the principal source of noise in my place is the furnace. The oil burner sounds like the space shuttle taking off. When we first moved in, that roar kept me awake at night: It was the sound of money burning up. Now that I'm accustomed to paying for warmth, I don't mind so much. In fact, the sound of the oil burner comforts me now. On the three or four nights each winter when the power goes out and the oil burner shuts down, the silence becomes so loud that it sometimes wakes me. It's dark and I'm cold; why can't I hear the furnace? During a big snowstorm last winter, I woke up in the middle of the night feeling mildly anxious, envisioning a cold house plumbed with frozen pipes. Would I have to trudge into the snow to fire up my generator? Then I heard the oil burner kick in. I smiled and fell back asleep.

During the summer, the house makes different noises. The big beams creak as the old house warms up during the day, and they creak as it cools down at night. A cricket moves into our living room and makes a sound that never seems to be coming from anyplace I look. The wind turns a screen door into a kazoo. Swallows sing in the chimney. Baby bats squeak behind the shutter outside the window in the third-floor bathroom. Deer walk quietly but munch audibly as they level the yew bushes on either side of the back door.

My children like to sleep with their doors open at night. Far from keeping them awake, the noises of the house make them feel safe like an auditory night-light. Is there any sound more portentous than absolute silence? Like my children, I am lulled to sleep by the hum of domestic machinery, and by the sound of a well-trained puppy snoring softly near my feet.

# Sliding Through Winter

L ATE ON A SNOWY NIGHT, I was out shoveling my driveway when my friends Rex and Polly came churning up our steep dirt road in Rex's four-wheel-drive car. Rex loves traction, and when a big snowstorm hits, his first thought is to go for a drive. Our road is one of his favorite proving tracks, because negotiating it can be tough in nice weather. They pulled over to chat. We went inside for a nightcap, then decided to go sledding. Rex's tire tracks made a perfect luge course. We started up near our mailbox, at the top of the hill, and ran all the way down to a little bridge at the bottom. With each run the course got faster. The fun lasted until the town snowplow appeared a little after midnight and covered our course with sand.

When I was a teenager, my friends and I used to sled on a steep suburban street not far from my parents' house. On bitterly cold Friday nights, a friend's older brother would use a fireman's wrench (which he had acquired under mysterious circumstances) to open a hydrant at the top of the hill, and we would sled all weekend on the resulting sheet of ice—our private glacier. Stopping was tricky. The street emptied into a busy avenue at the bottom of the hill, and the only way to avoid it was to yank your sled into a driveway just short of the intersection. One year I lost part of a front tooth when a friend and I crashed full speed into a curb. Each of us had the other in a headlock. The jagged edge of my broken tooth was red. The red was an exposed nerve, I thought, but the dentist, after a little painless probing, determined that it was paint from my Flexible Flyer.

Not far from that street was a huge vacant lot. One summer we cut a winding path through the woods. The following winter we spent long afternoons banking the turns with densely packed snow. Our sled run spilled out of the woods and across the backyards of several neighbors. One afternoon my friend Duncan missed a turn, crashed through the shrubbery, and slit the top of his left hand from the tip of his index finger to his wristwatch. The cut required many stitches and a long rehabilitation, but Duncan was back on his sled before the winter ended.

A few years ago my children and I discovered that we could sled alongside our road in a narrow trough created by the town plow. We had to trim a few branches and remove some huge stones that scraped the bottoms of our sleds. We got rid of the stones by digging them out with a long pry bar, rolling them into my wife's old flying saucer, and sending them skidding down the road to the bottom of the hill. That's pretty much the same way New England farmers in the olden days dealt with the largest boulders in their fields: they waited until winter, then used oxen to drag them across the ice.

My kids and I are always anxious as we wait for the first big snow of this season. Some years we have very little snow, and that thought makes the kids nervous. We pass the time by using my pry bar and loppers to do preliminary maintenance. We trim the blue spruce tree near the mailbox. We move a few of the nastier-looking stones. Then we stare for a while at the gray sky and go back inside to check the Weather Channel.

# Protector Hats

ALMOST EVERY SHOW ON TELEVISION, including the news, has parts that are too embarrassing for normal people to watch. On *L.A. Law,* for example, Mr. Sifuentes once had a romantic dinner with a pretty dentist who had retained him, just before injecting him with Novocain, to represent her in a malpractice suit that had been filed by a patient who believed that she (the dentist) had installed a tiny radio in her (the patient's) mouth.

That wasn't the embarrassing part. The embarrassing part came after the romantic dinner, when the dentist said in a sexy voice that she was going to do something very special for Mr. Sifuentes. Then, suddenly, she was straddling Mr. Sifuentes and using some sort of dental equipment to clean Mr. Sifuentes's teeth. While she was doing that, she was saying—

Naturally, I have no idea what she was saying. The whole time she was saying it, I was saying, *"Buh buh buh"* and poking my fingers in and out of my ears. I bet there aren't ten people in America who know what that dentist said to Mr. Sifuentes.

If you're watching a movie on a VCR, you can fast-forward through the embarrassing parts. But you can't do that with ordinary television, unless you videotape everything and then watch the tape. When the embarrassing parts come on, you have to run out of the room, sing in a high voice, eat a big mouthful of potato chips, or say, *"Buh buh buh"* and poke your fingers in and out of your ears. Or wear a protector hat.

I invented the protector hat one night while my wife and I were watching *Moonlighting* and folding the laundry. It was that terrible episode in which Maddie and David speak in fake Shakespearean English and act out a sort of parody of *The Taming of the Shrew,* complete with period props and costumes. There were so many embarrassing parts that blocking out all of them would have made it impossible to fold the laundry. I tried shaking my head back and forth rapidly, to distort my hearing, but that gave me a headache.

Then I had an idea. I took a folded dish towel and put it on my head. I could still see and hear the show—I didn't cover my eyes or ears—but the embarrassing parts seemed less embarrassing. Objectively, a dish towel draped lightly on the head offers no protection from anything. And yet it helped. "Put on a protector hat," I said to my wife. "It helps."

With towels on our heads, we were able to watch the rest of the show. In very embarrassing parts, I would pull firmly on the ends of my towel, applying a protective pressure to the top of my head. In extremely embarrassing parts, I would stuff the ends of the towel between my glasses and my eyes. At times the show became so embarrassing that I wondered whether I would have to wear a protector hat for the rest of my life. But I made it through.

How do protector hats work? I don't know. Why does pulling a blanket over your head make it impossible for enemies from space to shoot you in your sleep? I don't know that, either. Perhaps it has something to do with the chemistry of the brain or certain properties of cloth. All I know is that it helps.

# Nature's Double Standard

OR YEARS AND YEARS, few people paid attention to the environmental consequences of home construction and renovation. Hardly anybody cared about the toxins in building materials, or the environmental stresses caused by the disposal of demolition debris, or the ecological arrogance of such rich-guy amenities as heated swimming pools and electric towel warmers. Many people behaved as though their electronically controlled thirty-two-head showers came first, while the earth came a distant last. More recently, though, a significant number of people have begun to behave somewhat more responsibly.

And yet, the entire question of environmental responsibility is a bit more complicated than it's usually given credit for being. Granted, we humans have been negligent. But what about the environment's behavior toward us? I mean, who started this?

Consider lightning. My water comes from a well. The well is a couple of hundred feet deep, and maybe eight inches in diameter. At the bottom of the well, hanging from the end of a long plastic pipe, is an electric pump. The pump hums along outside my consciousness, silently and reliably bringing water into my house. Or at any rate it did until one cold winter day, when I suddenly noticed that the powerful flow from the kitchen faucet had dwindled to a feeble, erratic stream. I called a plumber. He poked around in the basement for a while, then went outside and hauled up the pump. The plastic pipe stretched all the way up to the mailbox. The pump was DOA. "Lightning," said the plumber. The bill: a thousand dollars.

I was tempted to go back into the house and flush caustic liquids down the toilet, just to get even. Sure, lightning can be beautiful—even breathtaking. But there are costs as well. Isn't it a little late in the game for the environment to be flinging around high-voltage static electricity with what can only be described as sociopathic abandon? The risks have been well known for millennia. Obviously, someone has to pay. Recently, that someone was me.

Radon is another example. Experts say it's deadly, yet how many people actually believe them? You can't see, smell, hear, or taste radon. The only way to find it is to test for it, and the results of the tests can be ambiguous. So how are you supposed to become adequately concerned about it? I don't think this is a human problem. If the environment were playing fair—if it were doing no more than it expects of us—radon would be a stinky green gas or, even better, a bubbling purple liquid. You would see it seeping through the cracks in your basement, and without hesitation you would call someone to do something about it. As things now stand, I can't even seem to make myself go and buy one of those little testers.

I guess I sometimes feel as though the environment employs a double standard insofar as responsibility is concerned. I'm not supposed to put salt on my driveway, but it's fine for Mother Nature to build ice dams above my eaves. I spend roughly half of every winter tottering on a stepladder on the flat roof above my laundry room, trying to reach the peak of my house's main roof with my aluminum snow rake. Granted, shoveling snow off my roof is an aerobic activity. In fact, it's probably the only real exercise I get all winter. But I don't think it's fair for me to have to maintain a constant weather vigil just to keep water from leaking into the bedrooms of my children, who have a hard enough time falling asleep as it is. I mean, they're innocent little children, for goodness sake. Environmental responsibility is a two-way street.

# *Pfft*

I N MY MIND I AM SEVENTEEN, although in actual fact—in
man-years—I am older. When we used to need babysitters, I
thought of them as young contemporaries, the way eleventh-
graders think of ninth-graders. They, in contrast, thought of me as
a crumbling historical specimen. "I wish my dad would ever wear
a jacket like that," one of them told me once. She didn't mean (it
turned out) that she thought I looked sharp; she meant that she
wished her father would stop trying to dress so youthfully.

When I was twenty-five, I was walking down Seventieth
Street in New York wearing blue jeans, sneakers, and an old
sweatshirt. Two boys in their late teens were playing football on
the sidewalk. The ball got away from them and rolled to my feet.
I bent to pick it up and toss it back. One of the boys said, "I'll get
that, sir," as polite as if I had been eighty years old and offering to
ride over a waterfall in a barrel.

I got so used to being thought of as a member of the Young
Generation that the idea of becoming a member of the Old Generation has been hard to accept. That feeling seems to be widely
shared. Most people my age seem to teach their children to
address grown-ups by their first names. I am Dave or Davey to
my children's friends, not Mr. Owen. In fact, my own kids call
me Dave. They've been doing it since they were little, and I
haven't discouraged them. They refer to my wife and me as

"Mom and Dave," making us sound like a middle-aged woman and her gigolo—perfect. The first time my daughter called me Dave, I was as thrilled as I was when, at around the same time, I went to the front door of my house and a salesman asked, "Are your parents home?"

When my daughter turned two, I said to her, "Here's how old you are: one, two. Now here's how old Daddy is: one, two, three, four, five, six, seven, eight, nine, ten, eleven, twelve, thirteen, fourteen, fifteen, sixteen, seventeen, eighteen, nineteen, twenty, twenty-one, twenty-two, twenty-three, twenty-four, twenty-five, twenty-six, twenty-seven, twenty-eight, twenty-nine, thirty, thirty-one." That made me feel depressed. To make myself feel better, I told her how old Grandpa was.

When my daughter was born, one of her great-grandfathers said, "I don't mind being a great-grandfather, but I can't stand being the father of a grandfather."

When I was twenty-one, I asked my father, who was fifty-one, how old he felt. "Not very," he said. I asked, "How long does it seem since you were my age?" He thought for a moment, then waved his hand and said, *"Pfft."*

# Living by Woods

O
NE OF OUR NEIGHBORS when I was growing up was an old man with a messy backyard. The rear quarter of the yard was an overgrown tangle of bushes, weeds, and saplings that my friends and I called the Woods. It was not a forest. No matter where you stood in the Woods you were no farther than twenty-five feet from the nearest edge. But the Woods from the inside seemed like a wilderness. My friends and I set snares for animals, dug holes, fought wars, and built a hut like something out of *Tarzan*. In the Woods once, a poorly behaved boy from down the street pinned my sister's foot to the ground with a pitchfork. One of the rusty tines went all the way through the sole of her sneaker and into the dirt, miraculously passing between two of her toes.

The old man who owned the Woods died two or three years after we moved in, and a dentist bought his house. The dentist's unpleasant children viewed the Woods as theirs. We viewed the dentist and his family as a marauding colonial power and ourselves as conquered victims. Then the dentist's wife decided to garden, and my friends and I watched from my side of the fence as a man with a payloader cleared and leveled the rear of the yard. I don't think I had realized how small the Woods was until I saw it deforested. The sight of that tiny brown flower bed was a shock.

Today I live next to some real woods. When the old man who

owned them died, two or three years after we moved in, he bequeathed the land to a local preserve, which adjoined the other end of his property and already covered a couple of thousand acres. If you begin at the bottom of my driveway, you can walk three miles to an abandoned nineteenth-century railroad tunnel—which was cut through several hundred feet of rock at the rate of eight inches a day—and cross only one public road. Hikers seldom visit the part near my house, so my kids view it as their own. They call it the Woods.

A creek cuts through the Woods at the bottom of the hill on which our house stands. On the far bank lies a pile of stones that a hundred years ago was the foundation of a lumber mill. The remains of a second mill lie nearby, on another branch of the same creek. Near each ruined mill my children and their friends will sometimes turn up an old broken teacup, a rusted tangle of iron that was once a pair of scissors or a piece of a machine, or a century-old bottle that used to contain consumption medicine. One winter my son found the skeleton of a deer and brought home the skull, both antlers still attached.

The hill on the far side of the creek is crossed diagonally by a narrow road, which farmers must have used to bring timber to be sawn into boards. The road is overgrown with pricker bushes and small trees, but you can follow it almost all the way to the top of the hill. If you turn left at a point that my son has marked with a chunk of white quartz, you eventually come to the remains of a rectangular stone enclosure, about a dozen feet square. Similar enclosures are scattered through the Woods, always appended to old stone walls, and to us their original purpose is obscure. This one is of special interest because it served, twenty-five or thirty years ago, as the occasional home of a hermit, who was a former student at a nearby boarding school. My son and his friends peri-odically decide to restore the enclosure's collapsed roof, but after an hour or two of heavy lifting they inevitably look for a different project.

I like to watch the seasons change the Woods. In autumn, as the leaves come down, the big hill on the far side of the creek comes gradually into view, and it remains visible, like the scalp of a man with thinning hair, until May, when it begins to disappear again behind a wall of green. Every spring, I listen for the year's first veery, a bird whose call sounds like a slide whistle falling down a well. After a big rain, the creek runs so hard that you can hear it inside the house with the windows closed. One autumn my son watched a coyote chase and catch a rabbit. In the winter my kids and their friends put on snow pants and climb the frozen streams that truss the hillsides, then slide on their rear ends to the bank of the creek below. It's easy to find old tree trunks that have been mined by pileated woodpeckers. The birds, which look like miniature pterodactyls, are secretive and hard to spot, even though they're as big as crows. They peck rectangular holes the size of electrical-wiring boxes, and they work so slowly that each thud is distinct.

Living near a real forest sometimes makes me wish that I were nine again. The Woods across the road is exactly what I wished the Woods across the fence had been. But I didn't feel deprived as a child—until the day the payloader came. And after the payloader left, my friends and I found another wilderness to lose ourselves in, a weedy vacant lot down the street.

# Helpful Household Hints

I N THE EARLY EIGHTIES I appeared on the television show *To Tell the Truth*. I had just written a book to which Barry Manilow had optioned not only the movie rights but also the song rights. (The book was about a semester I had spent pretending to be a high school student.) On the show, only one of the panelists—it was Kitty Carlisle Hart—picked me from the lineup. I fooled Nipsey Russell, Rex Reed, and a fourth celebrity whose name I can't recall, and I won a hundred and fifty dollars in cash, a fifty-dollar gift certificate from a national shoe-store chain (which I redeemed for fifty pairs of white tube socks), a couple of other items, and some motor oil.

The most memorable thing about the day was not my winnings, however. It was meeting a contestant on another segment of the show, a woman named Poncé Cruse Evans, whom most people know as Heloise, of "Hints from Heloise." We chatted in the waiting room, and after a while I got up the nerve to tell her the only hint I had ever thought of by myself. "Did you know," I asked nervously, "that wearing a rubber glove makes it easier to open a jar?" She said, "Oh, yes," and quickly rattled off a dozen other uses for rubber gloves and a dozen other ways to open jars. As she was talking, I realized with sadness that no matter how many movies or songs Barry Manilow might make or sing about me (as it turned out, he didn't make or sing any), I sure didn't know many hints.

In the decade and a half since then, I have thought of quite a few hints. Well, not quite a few. But four. Here they are:

*To get rid of mice, keep rats.* We used to have a terrible problem with mice. They would wander through the drawers in our kitchen during the night, leaving a big mess. I accepted this with resignation. We live in the country, and I figured mice were part of the deal. But that was before we got rats.

My wife bought a pet rat a couple of years ago. Then, because the rat seemed lonely, she bought another. The second pet rat turned out to be pregnant, and soon, instead of having two rats too many, we had sixteen rats too many. We gave most of the ratlings away, but we kept several, and eventually we moved their huge cage into the basement. In a short time, our mouse problem disappeared.

Rats don't like mice. One morning we found half a mouse in the rats' cage. The mouse had squeezed through the bars during the night, probably thinking, "My rodent brothers will be happy to share their corn," and the rats had reacted the way thugs in a pool hall do when a wimpy guy carrying a violin case comes in to use the bathroom. The other mice got the message, and that was that.

Or so I thought for quite a while. Recently, though, while poking around in the basement, I discovered the real reason we don't have mice in our kitchen anymore: there is now so much mouse food in the basement—my wife keeps big bags of grain in a cupboard, for the rats—that the mice no longer bother to come upstairs. The basement is like a fabulous mouse resort with a twenty-four-hour-a-day all-you-can-eat buffet. That's okay with me. I don't mind sharing my house with animals, as long as they stay away from the silverware.

*To clean wet oil paint from your hands, use french fries.* If you have ever painted your shutters and then gone to McDonald's for lunch without bothering to clean up thoroughly, you may already know that turpentine and paint thinner aren't the only open-chain hydrocarbons that dissolve oil-based paints. Vegetable oil, lard, salad dressing, bacon grease, some kinds of hand lotion, Vaseline, and other substances do, too. I like to use corn oil to clean up my hands. It doesn't irritate my skin, the way paint thinner does, and it doesn't stink up the kitchen. It works best if you add a little dish detergent to it. Don't use corn oil to clean your paintbrushes, though, or you'll end up with a terrible mess.

*French fries aside, the most powerful cleanup tools you own are water and time.* Need to clean a roasting pan crusted with baked-on food? Pour water on it and walk away. Want to remove some ugly wallpaper from the family-room walls? Use a sponge to wet it down, and walk away. Tired of the coating of dirt that covers your car? Park it in the shade, spray it with a hose, and walk away.

Soaking is as powerful as scrubbing, and it's easier on your arms. Before breaking out the elbow grease, give the earth's most abundant solvent a chance to do your work for you. The trick is not to become impatient. Give the water enough time to work its magic. And anything that's left will probably come off with corn oil.

*To open a stubborn jar, grip the lid with a sheet of sandpaper.* This works even better than a rubber glove. The tiny pieces of grit act like thousands of powerful grippers, giving you enormous leverage. I don't remember how I discovered this, but I don't think I learned it from Heloise. She can have this hint for her column, though, if she wants it. I'm sure I can think of more.

# Notes from Underground

I VIVIDLY REMEMBER THE FIRST TIME I cleaned up my basement. It was four or five years after we moved in, at a little after two in the morning. I had just called the fire department to report that my wife and I had been awakened by the smell of smoke. After hanging up, I ran down into my basement to see if I could find the source of the smell. I found it in a plastic trash barrel: some linseed-oil-impregnated rags that I had thrown away the previous day. The rags had spontaneously combusted, and a thin plume of smoke was rising from them. I blasted the barrel with a fire extinguisher and carried it out into the snow. Then I ran back inside and, in the minute or two before the fire department arrived, frantically tried to straighten up my basement. There were fire and safety hazards everywhere, and I didn't want the fire chief to see them.

In the years since that night, my basement has returned to its prefire condition. There is only one small patch of unobstructed floor space. It is two feet wide and eight feet long, and it leads from the foot of the stairs to the door of the freezer. The rest of the floor is covered with the junk that I inexorably collect without exactly meaning to: pieces of molding that are too short to be of any conceivable use but too long to throw away; a broken lawn sprinkler that the previous owner didn't feel like taking with him when he moved away; fifteen or twenty feet of unrolled fiberglass insulation, a large leftover part from a project I don't remember; a dozen or so coffee cans with paintbrushes frozen like Popsicle sticks in the crud congealed inside them; every knob and hinge that I have ever removed from anything; a dozen nearly empty joint-compound buckets; a box containing all of the safety features that used to be attached to my table saw; about a hundred old doors.

The only things you won't find in my basement are my tools, which are scattered through the house. You can go into almost any room and, by taking an inventory of the tools abandoned there, quickly tell which project I'm in the process of not finishing.

My friend Rex has a basement you could store newborn babies in. Every tool is hanging from a hook, every cord is neatly coiled, every vaguely ambiguous container has a label. Rex is the sort of person who puts things away when he is finished with them. When he needs to cut a board in half, he doesn't have to rest one end of it on the router leaning against the vacuum cleaner lying on the broken dehumidifier in front of his sawhorse. He just rests it on his sawhorse. Needless to say, Rex is appalled by my basement, and every so often I am able to see it through his eyes. The last time that happened, I resolved to take a week off and make my basement look like his.

That was years and years ago. I still intend to do it, but I don't know how to begin. There might be a lever long enough to move all that stuff, but where would I find a place to stand?

# The Perfect House

L IKE EVERYONE ELSE, I live in an imperfect house. It has closets that are too small, a kitchen that is too old-fashioned, and a garage that is too full of broken bicycles, dead leaves, broken bricks, broken plastic wading pools, a broken gasoline-powered generator sitting in a broken red wagon, garbage cans, and garbage. Also, there is only one sink in my kitchen.

For the most part, I am resigned to my lot. I am old enough now to realize that my wife is probably never going to turn to me and say, "Darling, I've watched you carefully all these years, and I am now convinced that you really do love me for myself, and I am happy to tell you that I have a two-hundred-and-fifty-million-dollar trust fund that I never mentioned before." In all likelihood, we are now as rich as we will ever be, and I will never be able to afford a garage big enough to actually park cars in. Still, I sometimes like to think about how I would live if I could live any way I wanted to. The perfect house, I think, would have many perfect features, including the following:

• *A two-story basement.* My lower basement would contain all the stuff that's now in my regular basement. (We've reached the point where we simply throw things—such as empty coffee cans—down the basement stairs, which are so crowded with barbecue tools, old ice skates, and broken window screens that they are unsafe to walk on. Our basement is less a storage area than a small, interior landfill, now reaching capacity.) My upper basement would contain two bowling lanes, a squash court, a miniature-golf course, a movie theater, and so forth. The lower basement would be accessible by a freight elevator large enough to hold a pickup truck.

• *A drive-through kitchen.* Putting away groceries would be simpler if you could park next to the refrigerator. Ditto getting the kids to school on time: you could feed them right in the car. You might also want to be able to drive into the laundry room. That way, when you returned home from two weeks at the beach, you could unpack the car directly into the washing machine.

• *A separate, hermetically sealed wing for pets.* The pet wing would have stainless steel cages, stainless steel walls, and a stainless steel floor with a drain in the middle. It would have air-lock doors and a huge exhaust fan with a fur-and-feather filter. It would have an attached apartment for a full-time pet keeper, who would sing and read to our pets so that we would no longer feel guilty about never paying attention to them. There would be a big plate-glass window for viewing.

• *A subterranean family archive, with curator.* When a friend of ours realized that her house was on fire, last Christmas morning, she grabbed her children and her photo albums and ran out to the street. That's probably what I would do in the same situation. I am an inveterate scrapbook compiler, a trait I inherited from my mother. Sadly, I don't have enough time to do the job right. I've filled eight or nine big books so far, and I'm only up to 1995. What I need is a full-time scrapbook assistant—a graduate student from Yale, say—who would sift through my boxes of family snapshots, send away for reprints and enlargements, assemble scrapbook after scrapbook filled with amusing juxtapositions, edit out the boring parts of videotapes, and so on. This assistant would work all day in a climate-controlled vault and would periodically put together private shows with themes like "A Decade at the Beach" and "Happy Birthday to You." Our Christmas cards would always go out on time. We would never forget what our kids used to look like.

There would be a lot of other stuff, too, including a drinking fountain in every room and big boxes of money. But I could be reasonably happy with just the four items I've described. Acquiring them probably wouldn't even cost all that many millions of dollars. Darling, isn't there something you've been wanting to tell me?

# Moving On

I HAVE WRITTEN ABOUT the common human mental disorder that causes certain people to postpone fixing up their houses until shortly before putting them on the market. Potential buyers, these folks assume, are more discerning than they are, and thus could never be satisfied with lime-green carpet or a kitchen that lacks an isosceles work triangle. The paradoxical result is that a large portion of the nation's remodeling budget is spent in an effort to please total strangers.

You may have noticed that there is a related but distinct mental disorder: the tendency of certain people to put their houses on the market immediately after fixing them up. These are not people who remodel in order to make their houses more salable; these are people who remodel in order to make their houses more perfectly suited to themselves. Once they have done so, however, they suddenly develop wanderlust, and—without so much as a pinprick of remorse—they decide to abandon the gorgeous, costly dwellings that only a moment before they had viewed as their final resting places.

Reading the real estate section of my local paper recently, I noticed that three wealthy residents of my town have come down with this disease. All three own beautiful houses in which they have invested enough money to fund the state lottery for many weeks. All three until recently viewed their homes as personal

Xanadus. All three suddenly decided to sell—in each case, less than five years after building or moving in. One of these people, an acquaintance of mine, explained the decision to me in such an eerily matter-of-fact tone that I momentarily wondered whether an alien power had commandeered her cerebrum. Less than a year before, she had led me on a lengthy tour of her palace, lovingly describing the provenance of each expensive detail. Now she said, "It's just too big. We need a smaller place." In her voice there was no regret, and certainly no embarrassment. She talked about abandoning her dream house, on which the shingles had scarcely had time to weather, as though that were the only rational option.

In truth, I have suffered twinges of this malady myself. My wife and I have owned our house for a long time now. Room by room and dollar by dollar, we have gradually turned it into pretty much exactly the sort of place where we want to live. One recent accomplishment was finally finishing the dining room, which for five years had sat with bare Sheetrock and unpainted woodwork. I can now honestly say that my house, though hardly perfect, looks quite a bit like the house I would build if I were handed a piece of land and a blank check. We have changed the house to suit our lives. After all these years, it seems almost as much a part of the family as the dog.

So why did my wife and I suddenly begin to think that we might want to dump the place and move somewhere else? This happened when the paint in the dining room was still damp. A big house up the road had suddenly come on the market (less than two years after the owners had bought it and drastically remodeled it). The owners were asking for a huge amount of money, and the place wasn't exactly what we wanted, and swinging the deal would have made us feel poor for many years—but almost instantaneously we were burning with the desire to move. It's hard to say what would have happened if the house hadn't just as suddenly been taken off the market again. It was a full week before my pulse returned to normal.

The explanation may be that there is something chilling about the thought that one has put one's life in approximately its final order. Finishing your house feels a bit like finishing your grave: there's nothing left to do but repaint every seven to ten years and wait to topple over. Or maybe fixing up houses is like having babies. As soon as you've forgotten what it's really like, you want to do it again.

# Drip, Drip, Drip

L IKE A LOT OF PEOPLE who live in the Northeast, I often
spend the best part of the ski season scraping ice from my
dormers and trying not to fall off my roof. Not that falling
off my roof in the winter would be dangerous; with four feet of
snow on the ground, I could jump from the top of my chimney
and not twist my ankle, much less break my neck. But I've never
fallen. I've dangled from ladders and balanced on chunks of ice
the size of bowling balls, and I've spent almost as much time
looking in through my windows as looking out.

My kids are thrilled by all the big storms. For them, snow has
no downside. During one recent winter, school was called off as
often as it was held. They sledded on our road, dug a tunnel in
the ten-foot-high mountain the snowplow created at the edge of
our driveway, and made snow angels in the middle of the street
on Christmas Eve. After a few weeks of regular blizzards, they
even stopped bothering to watch the Weather Channel, so confident were they that fresh storms were coming.

I couldn't share their enthusiasm. My attitude toward winter
changed forever when I became the owner of a roof. When a big
storm hits, I don't run around the house laughing and singing,
the way they do. Instead, I pace nervously from room to room,
looking for signs of leaks.

Like most houses—and especially most very old houses—

mine has nowhere near enough insulation. When snow piles high on the roof, heat escaping from inside the house melts the bottom layer. Water trickles down the roof and refreezes when it reaches the roof's cold edge, forming an ugly frozen hump called an ice dam. As the dam grows larger, more and more water backs up behind it. With nowhere else to go, the water eventually works its way under the shingles and into the house.

Almost everything homeowners do to eliminate ice dams makes them worse. Electric heating cables don't melt ice dams; they just turn the roof's cold edge into a zigzag. (If you look closely at the roof of a house with a heating cable over its eaves, you'll notice that ice dams have reformed both above and below it.) Removing the snow with a shovel or a snow rake works only if you remove *all* the snow, all the way up to the ridge. (Removing just the snow over the eaves, as most people do, merely moves the cold edge higher up the roof and can actually make leaks more damaging, by pushing them farther into the house.) Getting rid of gutters, which many people incorrectly view as the cause of ice dams, does nothing but ensure a wet basement when the big thaw finally arrives.

The only way to get rid of ice dams once and for all is to use some combination of insulation and ventilation to make the roof as cold as the outside air. Ice dams simply can't form on roofs that aren't heated from below. That's why you don't see brown, harpoon-sized icicles stuck to the eaves of old barns, unheated toolsheds, or doghouses. (The brown is dirt from under the shingles or inside the walls.)

The only other way to eliminate ice dams is to get rid of all the snow. That's what I do with my shovels and rakes. Ripping out our eighteenth-century attic and cramming it full of fiberglass insulation would work better but would be a colossal chore that I can't even bear to think about. I have no doubt I'll spend next winter the way I've spent most recent ones: clinging to my ladder, watching the moon rise over my chimney, and wishing for an early spring.

# The Genetics of
# Home Ownership

A RESEARCHER AT HARVARD recently found that people who live in apartments have brains that are structurally different from those of people who live in houses. She suspects, furthermore, that the urge to buy and live in a house may be determined by the presence or absence of what she calls a "homeowner's gene." Her work may go a long way toward explaining why some people are comfortable shopping in hardware stores, while others can't seem to get through life without the assistance of a building superintendent.

Actually, I made all that up. As far as I know, all the differences between apartment dwellers and homeowners are environmental in origin. But the differences are real, as anyone who has closely observed the two groups can attest. I was reminded of this recently by the experiences of a friend of mine, a lifelong New York City apartment dweller who a couple of years ago bought a weekend house in the country. I'll refer to my friend as Julia (her real name).

Julia's troubles began almost the moment she took possession of her house. A big rainstorm filled one corner of her basement with water, and she called me in a panic, wondering what she ought to do.

"Maybe your gutters are clogged," I said.

"Should I call a lawyer?" she asked.

"To clean your gutters?"

"To sue the guy I bought this place from. The gutters are his responsibility, right?"

Last winter Julia called me with another water-related problem. A big ice dam had formed at the edge of her roof, and for several days water had been leaking into her living room through her big cathedral ceiling. Roof leaks are baffling to New York City apartment dwellers: There's no apartment up there, so where could the water be coming from? I explained ice dams to her and told her what I always tell people who complain about winter leaks: She needed more insulation and more ventilation under her roof.

To Julia, that sounded too complicated even to think about. Besides, the winter was almost over. But the next fall she began to worry about the cold weather that was coming, and on the night of the first freeze she called me again.

"All right," she said with determination. "Where do I buy some of this ventilation?"

I shouldn't have laughed, of course. If I moved to Manhattan now, I'd feel just as lost as she does in the country. Have you ever tried to fit Sheetrock into a taxi?

# Are Men Evil?

A FEW YEARS AGO, my wife noticed an apparent flaw in my character. She pointed out that if I had decided to (for example) replace the kitchen ceiling, I would invariably wait to begin until a day when we were expecting a dozen people for dinner. Quite naturally, I responded with anger and resentment.

On further reflection, though, I realized that she was right. I was able to confirm her observation one day when we were expecting thirty people for dinner. Caught up in the spirit of preparation, I decided to wax the living room floor, a chore that involved moving a lot of furniture and rolling up a big Oriental rug. The floor had needed waxing for some time, and a fresh coat would protect it from the feet of our guests. The only problem was that the feet of our guests were not going to come anywhere near the living room floor; the party was going to be held outside, on the patio and porch. Somehow my impulse to help had been channeled in the wrong direction.

Identifying a character flaw is not the same thing as eliminating it, as I learned the following Christmas. Christmas is one of the two or three times a year when we use our dining room as a dining room. During the rest of the year, we use it as a sort of combined warehouse and extra playroom—a purpose to which it is ideally suited, since it adjoins the kitchen and has a big table that the dog can't jump onto. In the spirit of the season, I decided to clear out all the extraneous stuff, revealing the dining room within. In fact, I decided to paint the walls and woodwork, which had been bare since the late eighties, when I ran out of steam on a major dining room renovation project after redoing the walls and installing some custom-milled moldings.

It was at that point that my thinking took a fatal (and, apparently, characteristic) detour. For several years, my wife and I had talked about replacing the dining table with a pool table, thereby giving the room a year-round purpose. Suddenly, this notion popped back into my head, and I decided that the first step in my cleanup operation ought to be shoring up the bouncy dining room floor, which is held up by two-hundred-year-old chestnut beams that by themselves would be incapable of supporting a pool table. In fact, the windows used to rattle when our dog—a dachshund—walked across the room. So I bought a bunch of two-by-sixes and built a stud wall in the basement directly under the beams. Doing that made the floor as solid as a parking lot. It also put another idea into my head: As long as I had one stud wall, why not build three more, creating the frame for a new room in the basement? The new room could hold a lot of the stuff that now clogs up the dining room, or it could be a sort of second playroom, or it could be a workshop for me, or it could be an in-home media center. Or something. But it would have Sheetrock and electrical outlets and wall-to-wall carpeting and all that other fun stuff.

I threw myself into the project like a man possessed, filling our minivan with load after load of lumber, and sawing and hammering late into the night. My progress was so swift that by Christmas morning I was nearly ready to apply the second layer of joint compound. In another year or two, no doubt, I'll have the place painted, and the kids and I will be spending many happy hours down there, doing whatever.

As for Christmas dinner, we ate it in the kitchen—a family tradition in the making. Doing the dishes was a snap, because the sink was right there. And the kids learned a valuable lesson about the true meaning of the season, which, after all, had its beginnings in a cow shed.

# Holiday Inspiration

THE TROUBLE WITH CHRISTMAS—

No, wait, scratch that.

A couple of years ago, entirely by accident, my wife and I made an important discovery about holidays. Our daughter was sick on Christmas morning, and after some anxious deliberation we decided to postpone the big, traditional feast that we had been planning for that evening. At first, the thought of having Christmas without Christmas dinner filled us with gloom. But as the afternoon wore on, our attitude changed. My wife didn't run to the kitchen to shell walnuts and baste the suckling pig. Our son started a Lego project on the dining room table and knew that he wouldn't be disturbed before he finished. Our daughter stretched out on the couch and read new books while the fire burned down in the fireplace. I didn't have to trade my pajamas for a sport coat. At some point, we sang "We Three Kings," using lyrics my wife's sister, at the age of seven or eight, laboriously printed out in crayon on a piece of red construction paper:

*We three kings of Orentar*
*Barring gifts we travel afar*
*Feild and foutain*
*Moor and mountain*
*Oo-ooo, star of wonder . . .*

The day dissolved in a pleasant way, and at bedtime every-one's blood pressure still registered in the normal range—a hol-iday first at our house.

We ended up having Christmas dinner a couple of days later, when our daughter was back on her feet. By that time, throwing a party for ourselves seemed like a fun idea. All the candy in the house had been eaten, so people were hungry again. Because there was no deadline, the preparations were relaxed, and doing the dishes afterward wasn't the last straw. Best of all, delaying dinner made Christmas seem to last longer than a nanosecond. We'll never have Christmas dinner on Christmas again.

Since then, we've found other ways to improve the holiday. For several years, we've devoted an afternoon to building a gingerbread house. (We don't really use gingerbread; we glue together a couple of cardboard boxes, then cover them with canned frosting and pieces of candy. Incidentally, you can make terrific stained glass by melting sour balls in the oven.) Finishing the house by Christmas was a stressful challenge, since con-struction inevitably had to be squeezed between a last-minute trip to the mall and a last-minute trip to the post office. But then we realized: Why not simply move the completion date to New Year's, or Valentine's Day, or Easter? Once the shroud of obliga-tion had been lifted, shingling a roof with Necco wafers seemed interesting again.

If you accept the idea that reducing holiday tension is a worthy goal, additional innovations are easy to think of. Christ-mas cards don't have to arrive before Christmas, or ever. (We're now many years behind.) There's no law that says you have to listen every year to your scratchy old recording of Dylan Thomas reading *A Child's Christmas in Wales*. If no one in your household even likes pecan pie, why make one? An invitation to a Christmas party is not a subpoena.

The trouble with Christmas is not that it's vulgar or over-commercialized; by this point, what isn't? The trouble with Christmas and other important holidays is that we let them get the better of us. We treat them like contests or final examinations rather than times of rest and reflection and joy.

There's a simple test for almost any holiday activity: When it's over, will our moods be better or worse? If you can stop gilding pinecones long enough to make yourself look at it that way, then the fact that your kids no longer feel like making seed balls for the chickadees may seem like less of a catastrophe.

# Little Town

A TOWN THE SIZE OF A HIGH SCHOOL has numerous unique features, among them amateur theatricals in which you know almost everyone in the cast. I don't go to many local plays, but I do attend the annual Christmas pageant, which for a number of years has been directed by my wife. She is a stickler for some details—my daughter, at the age of four, came home from rehearsal with a grim face and said, "Dave, I have bad news: the angel Gabriel is a boy"—but not for others. Every year a few children in the cast object to filling the usual roles, and my wife permits them to appear instead as whatever they were for Halloween. Over the years, the entourage in the stable in Bethlehem has included not only shepherds, angels, wise men, and sheep, but also a dinosaur, a monkey, a princess, a tree, a bee, and a pirate.

The baby Jesus is sometimes portrayed by a live baby and sometimes not, depending on the vintage of that year's crop of infants. One year Jesus was an anatomically correct male doll, which a forward-thinking aunt had given my two-year-old son (who named it Claudia) the Christmas before. Another year Jesus was a real three-month-old girl named Eleanor. During most of the pageant you could see her tiny hands moving back and forth above the sides of the manger. Among the animals that year was a fierce-looking tiger, who walked down the aisle of the church with a plastic chicken drumstick in his jaws. He presented the drumstick to Eleanor by leaning over the edge of the manger and opening his mouth. Later, Eleanor cried and was comforted by her seven-year-old sister, who was playing Mary. ("You are my puny wife," a much larger Joseph had told her before the show began.) When Eleanor continued to cry despite being patted forcefully on the stomach and having her sister's fingers jammed into her mouth, her real mother took her away, and she was replaced by her understudy, a rolled-up blanket.

The pageant makes a large and favorable impression on the participants. When my daughter was very young, she would come home intoxicated by both the applause of the audience and the grandeur of the script. She would pace back and forth in the playroom afterward, playing several parts herself and narrating her own versions of the story. In one of them, which I overheard from the kitchen, Jesus had "long pants, a royal coat, shoes made of wood, and long, straight socks." Later, she stood on the couch and pretended to read from her paperback copy of *Beezus and Ramona*, which served as her Bible:

> *The angel Gabriel appeared and told Mary she was going to have a baby.*
>
> *"But how can I have a baby?" Mary asked. "I don't have a husband."*
>
> *"Don't worry, my dear," said Gabriel. "You should have a husband." And the angel waved his wings and separately a husband appeared.*
>
> *"His name is Joseph," said the angel Gabriel. "I've got to fly to tell other mothers in the church Bible to have babies."*
>
> *And Mary said to her husband, "Dear, we're having a baby, and his name is going to be Jesus Christ the Lord."*

Long after the pageant ended one year, my kids and I put on our long pants and royal coats and walked back up to the village green. Snow had begun to fall earlier that day, and the storm was shifting into second or third gear. We saw no one else walking, and no cars. The church was dark, but through the windows of the houses of my neighbors we caught glimpses of the other pageant, the one that goes on all the time. My glasses were getting snowy, so I took them off. Viewed myopically, the windows looked shimmery and old-fashioned, and the streetlights had points like stars. We saw the town snowplow, whose driver honked hello, and the state snowplow, whose driver didn't. Then we found a snowbank under a hemlock tree next to the road, and we stretched out right there on the ground. We lay there for a long time, as the lights went out in some windows and came on in others, and we watched the snow come down.

# About the Author

David Owen was born in Kansas City, Missouri, in 1955. He has been an editor of the *Harvard Lampoon*, a fact checker for *New York*, a regular contributor to *Esquire*, a senior writer for *Harper's*, and a contributing editor of *The Atlantic Monthly*. He is currently a staff writer for *The New Yorker* and a contributing editor of *Golf Digest*. He lives in northwest Connecticut with his wife and their two children.